Jewells from My Journey

Devotionals for the Christian Walk

Lynn Milner

Jewells from My Journey: Devotionals for the Christian Walk
ISBN: Softcover 978-1-955581-41-7
Copyright © 2015 by Lynn Milner

All rights reserved. No part of this book may be reproduced or transmitted in any form or by any means, electronic or mechanical, including photocopying, recording, or by any information storage and retrieval system, without permission in writing from the publisher.

To order additional copies of this book, contact:
Parson's Porch Books
1-423-310-8815
www.parsonsporch.com

Parson's Porch Books is an imprint of Parson's Porch & Company (PP&C) in Cleveland, Tennessee. PP&C is an innovative non-profit organization which raises money by publishing books of noted authors, representing all genres. All donations from contributors and profits from publishing are shared with the poor.

Dedication

This devotional book is dedicated to Jewell Catherine McDonald Cassels. She was the godliest woman I have ever known. I had the privilege of calling her "Grandma."

My Grandma was named correctly by her parents. She was definitely God's jewel to me and my entire family.

Grandma possessed every fruit of the Spirit: love, joy, peace, patience, kindness, goodness, faithfulness, gentleness and self-control. (Galatians 5:22-23)

Jewell Cassels was an inspiration and a blessing to everyone who knew her. The first thing you would notice was her smile. She always had a beautiful countenance on her face. No one had sweeter cheeks to kiss than my Grandma.

Grandma would easily be brought to tears at the mention of her Savior's name. No one could ask the blessing, pray or read Scripture without her needing a tissue. She inspired me to love Jesus with all of my heart, soul, mind and strength. (Mark 12:30)

She would tell me not to make such a fuss about her and that she wasn't worthy of everything I have said. However, I would beg to differ.

It was fitting that at age 94, with her family gathered around her and singing her favorite hymns, she went home to be with her Savior on Palm Sunday 2014. She is greatly missed.

Acknowledgements

This book would not be possible or worth the paper it is written on, without my Savior and Lord, Jesus Christ! It is through His divine power and for His glory alone that I penned these devotionals. May He be glorified!

"Do not be afraid for I have ransomed you. I have called you by name; you are Mine. When you go through the deep waters, I will be with you. When you go through the rivers of difficulty, you will not drown. When you walk through the fire of oppression, you will not be burned up; the flames will not consume you. For I am the Lord, your God, the Holy One of Israel, your Savior." Isaiah 43:1b-3a

To contact Lynn, please email her at: milnerml@comcast.net.

Table of Contents

Dedication	2
Acknowledgements	4
Surrender	9
Empty Words	12
No Words Needed	16
Helping or Hurting	18
Lying Lips	21
When I am Afraid	24
The Lord is With You!	26
Do Not Be Afraid	28
The Lord is Good!	30
Faith in the Unseen	32
Step Out in Faith	34
Be Teachable	37
His Unfailing Love	39
Seeking Jehovah!	41
Seek Strength	43
Our Daily Bread	45
The Pursuit of Holiness	47
God's Mighty Power	50
Thank You, Lord!	53
Needs vs. Wants	55
Wisdom and Understanding	57
Integrity	60

All Have Sinned 63
Forgive, as You Have Been Forgiven 66
A Good Friend 69
Distractions of Life 72
Dedicated to the Lord 75
Rest and Relaxation! 78
Watching and Waiting 80
He Sustains Me! 81
Press On 84
All Will Become Clear 85
Follow Me 87
Calling 89
Steps Secured 92
Go to the High Places 94
The Plan 97
He's Got the Plan! 100
Be Still and Know 102
Author and Perfecter 104
I Want to be Blessed! 107
The Battle Begins in the Mind 109
It is by Grace! 112
Freedom From Opinion 114
A New Creation 116
Laughter Hides the Pain 119
We are not Orphans 122
Love One Another 124
Control Freak! 126
But I Prayed About It! 129
Exhausted 133
Spiritual Exercise 134
We are Weak, but He is Strong 136

Technical Difficulties! 139
Strength for Our Sorrows 141
My Help Comes From the Lord! 143
Feeling Overwhelmed? 145
It's Gonna' Get Better 147
Be Patient, The Lord is Coming! 150
RESOURCES 152

Surrender

I deliver up myself
to the Lord.

Surrender

Surrender in Greek is **ekdotos**. Phonetic Spelling: (ek'-dot-os) Definition: given up, delivered up.

Derived from the Greek root words **ek** and **didomi Ek** has a two-layered meaning, which is **"out from and to."** *Didomi* means **"I offer, I give; I put, I place."** (Strong's Exhaustive Concordance)

So the exact Greek translation for the word **Surrender** is: **Out from (inside me); to (the Lord); I offer (give, put, place) myself. - I am delivering myself up to the Lord from the inside out.**

This reminds me of the song, From the Inside Out by Hillsong. There is a part of this song that stirs me every time I hear it.

> *My heart and my soul, I give You control*
> *Consume me from the inside out, Lord*
> *Let justice and praise, become my embrace*
> *To love You from the inside out*
> *Your will above all else, my purpose remains*
> *The art of losing myself in bringing you praise*

Many people have asked me why I chose to name this ministry, Surrendered & Free. It would take longer than I have time to write to give you the complete answer. However, the abbreviated answer is that the Lord asked for my surrender. When I did some digging into what that exactly meant, I was brought to my knees with both the realization that this was my only path to freedom from bondage, and it was also my deepest desire.

My heart would never be at peace until I was willing to give all of myself to the Lord. The beautiful thing I discovered is that I don't have to do this in my own power. God is the one who creates the desire to surrender to Him and gives me the power to do it. All I am required to do is yield my will to Him and allow Him to do His work in me. For it is God who is producing in you both the desire and the ability to do what pleases him. Philippians 2:13

Have you felt the Lord tugging at your heart to surrender to Him? Does this thought overwhelm you? Are you unsure exactly how to go about beginning this journey of surrender? It all starts with a willing heart and a request from you to the Lord, asking Him to help you give yourself to Him completely. He is faithful – He will answer.

Lord,
With each passing day – moment by moment – please help me give up my life in complete surrender to You and You alone!
Amen.

The *Power* of Words

Heavenly Father, please
bridle my tongue.

Empty Words

The lips of the righteous nourish many. Proverbs 10:21

Have you ever given serious thought to the words that flow out of our mouths so easily? Our words can either speak life or death, truth or lies, encouragement or gossip.

We have a choice each time we open our mouths as to whether we will allow the Holy Spirit to have control over our tongue or not. If we will give the Lord full control of our mouth, He can use it as a tool to bless those around us.

Recently I heard a well-known teacher make the point that sometimes our words are empty. Often we say things like: "Have a blessed day," or "I'll be praying for you." Maybe we mean well, but this teacher pointed out that no matter how much we tell others to have a blessed day, it isn't going to make them feel blessed. Another author made the observation that we speak empty words of blessing in order to absolve ourselves of any inconvenience of having to act on another's behalf. OUCH! My toes feel stepped on! Sometimes God is calling us to be a blessing in someone's life.

Is there someone God has placed on your heart to be a blessing to? Maybe He is asking you to take part in their life and meet a specific need through some act of kindness. Let me encourage you to ask God how you can be a blessing to someone today.

Lord,
May I look for the ways You want to use me in others' lives? Please make my words matter and not be full of emptiness. Help me be a blessing and not just speak words of blessing.
Amen.

Too Much Talk

To answer before listening — that is folly and shame.
Proverbs 18:13

Too much talk leads to sin. Be sensible and keep your mouth shut.
Proverbs 10:19

"Please, do not answer the question before you hear the question." These are the words I recently spoke to my teenager. She is often ready to give a defense for an action or request before I have even opened my mouth. (Parents of teenagers are probably saying a hearty, "Amen!")

It is easy for all of us to fall into this trap at times. We think we know what the other person is going to say so, we answer before listening. We speak out of turn, interrupt or talk over someone. These are annoying habits I am often guilty of.

We have heard it said that God gave us one mouth and two ears for a reason. He intended for us to listen twice as much as we speak. I can say with certainty, that my life would be much easier if I would take this lesson to heart!

Let us know that when we speak too much it can easily lead us to sin.
Proverbs 10:19

My paternal grandfather, (Papa), was very good at listening more than he spoke. When he actually did talk, everyone quieted to hear what he had to say. What he said was usually funny, wise or sometimes a bit of both. I learned some valuable life lessons from my Papa. He used a famous quote by Abraham Lincoln, **"Better to remain silent and be thought a fool than to speak and remove all doubt."**

Lately, I have been thinking a lot about my words. If my desire is for the words I speak to be anointed and used by God, then I must let the Lord have TOTAL control of my mouth. I must listen more and speak less. I must surrender my tongue to God's bridle.

There are many Scriptures on the taming and the power of the tongue. We would be wise to heed their instruction.

Lord,
Help me to listen more and speak less. Please, help me surrender my tongue to Your control. Anoint my words so that they may be a blessing to others. Amen.

No Words Needed

And the Holy Spirit helps us in our weakness. For example, we don't know what God wants us to pray for. But the Holy Spirit prays for us with groanings that cannot be expressed in words. Romans 8:26

The prayer concerns were many and the pain of some of them seemed almost unbearable. My heart was heavy and it seemed the words would not come - just tears.

So, I visualized myself curling up in the lap of my Savior and crying for a while. I poured my heart out to Him with my tears and rested in the knowledge that He knew what every one of them meant. He knows my heart. He understands every pain. He intercedes for me with groanings that cannot be expressed in words. That is comforting to me.

I have the gift of gab and there are very few times I am at a loss for words. However, I felt that quietness was a better choice in this moment. Meditation on God's Word and silent time spent with my Savior was greatly needed – not my words.

Some people are uncomfortable with silence, but silence can be a good thing. One major benefit is we can hear more clearly. Who can hear the still small voice speaking while we are busy talking? Doesn't the scripture say for us to "Be still and know that I AM GOD"? It doesn't tell us to rush around chattering and know that He is God. It says "BE STILL"!

Maybe you need to curl up in your Savior's lap and cry for a while, or just rest there for a time. Our words are not always needed. Basking in His presence, knowing that He hears, He sees, and He intercedes to our Heavenly Father on our behalf is all that is necessary.

Lord,
Thank You for allowing me to just rest in Your presence as You intercede for me.
Amen.

Helping or Hurting

It's better to live alone in the corner of an attic than with a quarrelsome wife in a lovely home. Proverbs 21:9

It is better to live alone in the desert than with a quarrelsome, complaining wife. Proverbs 21:19

A quarrelsome wife is as annoying as constant dripping on a rainy day. Stopping her complaints is like trying to stop the wind or trying to hold something with greased hands. Proverbs 27:15-16

A wise woman builds her house, but a foolish woman tears it down with her own hands. Proverbs 14:1

Do your toes hurt? Mine have been stepped all over as I read these verses. My husband said he would not describe me as a "quarrelsome wife." Opinionated – yes, but not usually quarrelsome. However, there have been times that I have become fixated on an issue. I had a difficult time letting it go until I felt that I had been heard, clearly understood and often agreed with. It is a good thing that the Lord is patient and longsuffering because I am a work in progress! Do I hear any "Amens"?

One night I was having one of those "fixated" moments. I mean, I was really going at it. All of a sudden, my husband looked at me and said, "Lynn, I feel like you are just looking for something to fight about." When I took a step back, I realized that the problem was not really the content of what I was saying. It was the delivery. I sounded angry and aggressive with my point of view. You can have a valid point without delivering it in an unkind way.

Recently, I read some biblical commentary on the word quarrelsome. It states, **"Quarrelsome nagging, a steady stream of unwanted advice, is a form of torture. People nag because they think they're not getting through, but nagging hinders communication more than it helps. Examine your motives. Are you more concerned about yourself – getting your way, being right – than about the person you are pretending to help? If you are truly concerned about other people, think of a more effective way to get through to them." (Tyndale – Life Application Study Bible)**

Sometimes we think we are trying to help those that we love by giving "unwanted advice." However, it may be seen as "a form of torture" to them. Have you ever looked into the eyes of your husband, child or friend and noticed that glazed-over look. That look is saying, "I tuned you out a long time ago, and I am begging you to stop!"

Two of the words in the dictionary used to define quarrelsome were bitter and choleric. When I looked up the word choleric in the dictionary, the definition stated; "Abounding with, or producing, bile." No wonder the Scripture speaks so strongly about a quarrelsome wife! She can make you sick! We expect our husbands to be Prince Charming, but do you think Prince Charming wants to come home to someone whose attitude and words sicken him?

The Scripture tells us that the power of the tongue is mighty. It holds the power of life and death. My sister taught her children this lesson by saying to them, "Are your words helping or hurting?" We would all do well to heed that advice.

Let's take the time to think before we speak, and ask God to put His bit in our mouth that will control our tongue. May we use it to build up, rather than to tear down.

Lord,
Please forgive me for the times I have been quarrelsome. Help me to control my tongue, and use it to bring blessings to others, rather than hurt. If I start to speak outside of Your will, please stop me in my tracks! Thank You for Your patience!
Amen.

Lying Lips

The Lord detests lying lips, but he delights in people who are trustworthy. Proverbs 12:27

Recently, I had to deal with several people who lied to me. One person promised they would do something they really had no intention of doing and ended up getting caught in that lie. Another person lied about going behind my back and doing something they promised they wouldn't do. Last but not least, someone lied to someone I love and hurt them tremendously.

When I shared all of this with my husband, I explained that I felt like someone had punched me in the stomach. It felt like I had been in a boxing match! Spiritual warfare at its finest!

All of this really made me think long and hard about how much our words matter – especially to the Lord. Some versions of this verse state that the Lord hates lying lips. That's a strong word. We'd like to think that we don't lie, but sometimes we embellish the truth or omit some facts to make the story sound better and get a laugh. Let's face it, we've all done it.

We take it to a whole new level when we start promising things and don't follow through, or give our word to someone, only to go back on it later. The Lord does not bless this behavior. I want the Lord to delight in me and find me trustworthy. I want my friends to have confidence that they can trust me. I don't want to have a reputation as a liar.

Do you find yourself having difficulty telling the truth? Do you embellish to make yourself look good to others? Do you justify your actions instead of owning them? These are questions we must ask ourselves.

If anyone thinks himself to be religious, and yet does not bridle his tongue but deceives his own heart, this man's religion is worthless. James 1:26

Did you know that the bridle for a horse contains several pieces? The bridle has a bit that is placed in a horse's mouth behind the teeth in the soft tissue of the gums. The noseband runs across the top of the nose and attaches to the bit. I find it interesting that the noseband is specifically used to keep the mouth closed. The entire bridle is connected to the reigns and is used to give the horse direction. I think we would all benefit by having the Lord's bridle controlling our mouths.

Lord,
Please place Your bit in my mouth and direct my speech to be pleasing to You. When others deceive me or hurt me with their words, may I forgive them, pray for them and remember, I too am a sinner saved by Grace. Amen.

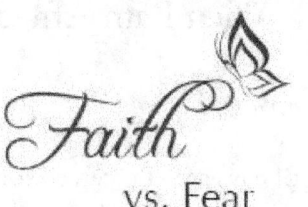
Faith
vs. Fear

When I am afraid,
give me Jesus.

When I am Afraid

When I am afraid, I put my trust in You. Psalm 56:3

A couple of days ago, I received some news that caused me to feel fearful. I tried to talk myself out of the fearful feelings. I thought about all the blessings in the middle of the adversity. I tried to be positive when I spoke about it. I really tried not to cry, even when I was alone. Does anyone see a pattern besides me? "I tried…" In my own power, I was trying to handle it.

A good friend said, "Lynn, you are human. You're allowed to feel afraid about this. The question is, what are you going to do with that fear? Are you going to try to handle it on your own, or take it to the One who can handle it for you?"

I love that this verse says, "When I am afraid…" I have made the big mistake of thinking that if I really loved and trusted God, I shouldn't have fear. Don't get me wrong, I think there is a serious faith crisis if we live in fear. However, experiencing the feeling of fear is completely normal. Just as my friend pointed out, it's what we do with it that matters.

I love the song entitled, "Give Me Jesus," by Jeremy Camp. I have decided to put the word, "afraid" in his lyrics. (Don't report me for plagiarism.) I have been singing to myself, "When I am afraid, Oh, when I am afraid, when I am afraid, give me Jesus."

As I was kissing my teenage granddaughter goodnight, she took my face in her hands and said, "Nana, I can tell that you are worried about this situation, but you need to remember, God has this." Very true!

Maybe you are facing a situation that is causing you to feel afraid. Don't try to deal with it alone. Meditate on this verse and take your fears to the Lord. In the words of my granddaughter, "God has this!"

Lord,
Please forgive me for trying to handle my fear by myself. I give it to You, Lord. Thank You for Your peace and the knowledge that You are trustworthy.
Amen.

The Lord is With You!

For The Lord your God is living among you. He is a Mighty Savior. He will take delight in you with gladness. With His love, He will calm all your fears. He will rejoice over you with joyful songs. Zephaniah 3:17

As I went through my typical morning routine, I turned on Pandora to listen to Praise Music. To my amazement, the song, "Give Me Jesus" by Jeremy Camp came on! I cried tears of joy! I felt that was God's gift to me having just written the previous devotional the day before. It was His reminder that He IS with me.

As the day progressed, I felt His presence with me. In the midst of my struggle to surrender my fear, He sent Christian clients to my salon to encourage and intercede for me. He "loved" on me through His people.

Wednesday night, after much comparison shopping, I finally decided to buy a tablet online. I've never had one and really needed it for work and ministry. My husband Mark knew I wanted one but happened to be asleep when I bought it.

When I got home from work Thursday, Mark said, "I won something today at work. I know you don't have a tablet yet, but I know you hope to have one someday so, I thought I would give this to you." It was a soft protective cover for a tablet. I started to cry. He said, "Why are you crying?" I told him that I ordered a tablet Wednesday night and as I was going to bed, I thought, "I don't have a protective cover for it? Oh well, I'll deal with that later." When Mark handed me that cover, it was just like God said, "Here, Lynn, I knew you needed this. Remember, I AM with you."

I love this verse in Zephaniah! I have always loved the part about God singing over me. The thought of that makes me want to dance. However, I was now drawn to the other portions of this Scripture.

In other versions, the first part reads, "The Lord your God is in your midst." I love that! He is always with me! It goes on to say, "He is a Mighty Savior." Yes He is! He is fighting my battles for me, and He has already won the war! The next part states that He delights in me. The God of the universe delights in me! God loves His children! Last but not least, "With His love, He will calm all your fears." He loved on me today and let me know that He sees to every detail of my life – right down to a cover for my new tablet! He knows what I need before I do!

If you are in the midst of a struggle between faith and fear, take the time to meditate on this verse and be reminded of the Mighty God we serve! I pray the Lord will calm your fears with His love.

Lord,
Thank You for Your presence with me! You are a Mighty God! I am blessed to know that You delight in me and sing over me! Please continue to calm my fears and comfort me with Your love.
Amen.

Do Not Be Afraid

The angel said to her, "Do not be afraid, Mary; you have found favor with God. You will conceive and give birth to a son, and you are to call him Jesus. He will be great and will be called the Son of the Most High. The Lord God will give him the throne of his father David, and he will reign over Jacob's descendants forever; his kingdom will never end."
Luke 1:30-33

Have you ever noticed that when God comes to His people to tell them that He has a big task for them, He tells them to not be afraid? I don't personally think this is just because an angel appears to them. I think it might also be because the task they were being asked to perform seemed overwhelming.

It is hard for me to imagine all of the doubts and fears that Mary must have been feeling and wrestling with as she heard the words the Angel spoke to her. The next nine months must have been extremely challenging. Do you think there was ever a time (maybe many) that she thought, I am the wrong woman for this job – I can't do this – it's too much!

Over my lifetime, I have felt those feelings and said those very words to the Lord – recently in fact. Every time He has asked me to do something that seems too hard or way beyond what I feel capable of doing, I hear His still small voice that reassures me and tells me not to fear. In fact, if I thought I could do what He is instructing me to do in my own power, I have a much bigger problem!

Are you facing circumstances that seem overly challenging and too difficult for you to handle? Do you feel as though God must have made a mistake when He called you to do something? Well, God doesn't make mistakes and if He called you to do it, He will equip you to do it.

I think He calls us to do things we cannot possibly do in our own power so that we may experience Him in a new way and others will see God's power revealed. Can you imagine what other women felt about Mary? Can you imagine what the disciples felt towards her? I can only imagine what respect and honor the believers who knew her must have had for her. She walked every day by faith.

I realized that God equipped Mary to carry, birth, raise and ultimately watch her son be crucified. Therefore, I must trust that He will equip me to do whatever He asks me to do.

As you face the challenges of the callings in your life, I pray the Lord will comfort you, guide you, protect you, and equip you. Do not be afraid; you have found favor with the Lord or He would not have called you to the task.

Lord,
Please help me to not fear and depend on You to equip me for the task.
Amen.

The Lord is Good!

Taste and see that the LORD is good; blessed is the one who takes refuge in him. Psalm 34:8

But Moses told the people, "Don't be afraid. Just stand still and watch the LORD rescue you today." Exodus 14:13

At the start of this day, I had no idea it would end the way it did. I had resolved myself to the fact that what I had hoped would come to fruition was just not going to happen. In my prayer time, I told the Lord I wanted only His will to work out in my life and if this was not His will – I didn't want it. I knew that if what I was hoping for worked out, it was only because the Lord caused it to happen.

In the last few days, the very things I write about and profess to believe were put to the test. Would I live out my faith and trust God or would I get upset and try to control the situation? The Lord gave me a clear sense that I was to stand still and wait on Him. I did as He asked and trusted Him to work it out.

In the eleventh hour, God worked out the circumstances as only He can, and what I had hoped for turned out far better than I could have ever thought possible. Little details fell into place within just a couple hours that had seemed impossible earlier in the day. Once again, God proved Himself faithful and reminded me just how awesome He is!

Do you have a circumstance in your life that seems hopeless? Does it look like there is no way it can work out? I am sure God's people felt that way when they were in captivity to the Egyptians. Moses tells them they will not have to fight to be set free. They are to stand still and watch the Lord rescue them.

I believe that the Lord is making it clear to us through His word that we should not try to fix, work out, manipulate, or attempt to control the circumstances in our lives. We need to just get out of His way and let God be God!

I am not suggesting that we sit on our hands in every situation life brings us. I am saying that when you have prayed, listened and done what you believe God has instructed you to do – it is time to stand still and wait on Him.

He didn't need my help creating the Heavens and the Earth. He didn't need my help with the plan of Salvation and hasn't asked for me to plan the Second Coming of Christ, so why is it I think He needs my help with the plans of my life? He's got this! God is truly in control. I'm not! Praise be to God!

Lord,
Thank You for Your unfailing love and provision in my life! I have tasted and seen that You are Good!
Amen!

Faith in the Unseen

Now faith is the assurance of things hoped for, the conviction of things not seen. Hebrews 11:1

"Faith proves to the mind, the reality of things that cannot be seen by the bodily eye." (Matthew Henry's Concise Commentary)

"Nana, how do I really know God is real, if I can't see Him?" This was one of those late night "let- me- stall- going- to bed" questions my granddaughter asked me. Due to the late hour, I gave her a brief description of what faith meant, and then told her we would talk more about it the next day. This gave me time to think and then better explain it to her.

As I pondered her question, I realized that it is a question that every Christian – if they're honest – has asked at least once in their faith journey. What if God is not real? What if Jesus isn't real? What if all this has just been some big lie? This is where faith comes in.

Everything in this earthly experience is all about our senses – what we can see, touch, hear and smell. We want proof of everything – video if possible. Faith, however, is about having a godly confidence in the things we cannot see. God's Word calls us to exercise our God-given faith. Where we lack faith, we should ask for increase. God is always ready to reveal Himself to those who are genuinely seeking Him. (See Jeremiah 29:13)

If you are in a faith crisis and you are just not sure if all you have believed is really real, ask God to increase your faith and reveal Himself to you in a new way today.

Lord,
Please increase my faith in You. Please help me to have total confidence in the things I cannot see and do not understand. I trust You, Lord. Help me trust You more.
Amen.

Step Out in Faith

Shortly before dawn Jesus went out to them, walking on the lake. When the disciples saw him walking on the lake, they were terrified. "It's a ghost," they said, and cried out in fear. But Jesus immediately said to them: "Take courage! It is I. Don't be afraid." "Lord, if it's you," Peter replied, "tell me to come to you on the water." "Come," he said. Then Peter got down out of the boat, walked on the water and came toward Jesus. But when he saw the wind, he was afraid and, beginning to sink, cried out, "Lord, save me!" Immediately Jesus reached out his hand and caught him. "You of little faith," he said, "why did you doubt?
Matthew 14:25-31

"Where is your faith, Lynn? Remember the pastor's sermon Sunday?" This was the question my husband asked me.

I was facing a new challenge in my life and in that moment my faith was weak. I was acting like it was my job to take this on in my own power! How arrogant!

On Sunday our pastor preached a sermon using this text in Matthew. It made a huge impression on me. The pastor made the point that Peter asked Jesus to call him out of the boat. Jesus calls him. However, did you notice that the storm was still going on? I never thought about it before. Jesus calls Peter to step out in a storm! Peter was doing fine until he took his eyes off of Jesus and focused on the storm. It was then that he started to sink.

Sometimes we ask to be used by God, but then we want it to be smooth sailing. No storms, please – peaceful waters only!

That's not the way life goes. We will encounter storms, but if we keep our eyes on Jesus, we will not sink. We can, (figuratively speaking), walk on water and do great things through the power of the Holy Spirit, and for the glory of the Lord.

Lord,
Help me to realize that you are where my total focus should be. You are in charge and You alone direct my steps. May I follow where You lead me, even in the midst of the storms of life.
Amen.

Seek the  *Lord*

Seek His face
continually.

Be Teachable

All Scripture is inspired by God and is useful to teach us what is true and to make us realize what is wrong in our lives. It corrects us when we are wrong and teaches us to do what is right. 2 Timothy 3:16

Recently someone asked me why it was important to read the Bible. I didn't want to give them a glib answer such as, "Because it's God's Word to us and He said we should read it." This is certainly true but seemed a bit trite when I felt this person really wanted to understand the Bible's importance.

I explained that it is important to read God's Word because it teaches us about His character and helps us to live a life that glorifies Him. The Bible is helpful when making decisions and trying to figure out what is right from wrong in a world where Christian values struggle to exist.

I once heard the pastor ask our congregation how often we read our Bibles. He asked if Sunday was the only time we picked up our Bible all week. He went on to ask, "If life was not going so well for you or you were confused about some situation, to whom or to where do you turn when you need answers?"

If we're not turning to the Lord in prayer AND not spending time in His Word, then we must be turning to human wisdom and self. Not a good choice!

The Bible is God-inspired, God-breathed and completely trustworthy! God's Word is absolutely necessary in order to understand God's will. May I be so bold as to submit a possible reason for not desiring to read God's Word?

Look at the verse above. Maybe we don't want to be corrected. Maybe we are comfortable in our current state and we don't want to hear what God has to say to us because we might have to change something – give up something – surrender something.

Let me encourage you to get into God's Word each day. Be teachable and see where God takes you. The journey is worth far more than what you think it will cost you.

Lord,
Please help me to be in Your Word every day, without fail.
Amen.

His Unfailing Love

Satisfy us each morning with your unfailing love, so we may sing for joy to the end of our lives. Psalm 90:14

Unfailing – never changing or becoming weaker even in difficult times; always providing enough of what is needed.

This verse is taken from one of the oldest prayers recorded in Scripture. Psalm 90 is Moses' prayer for the Israelite nation. In this verse several points of truth stand out.

First, only God's unfailing love (never changing – always enough) can satisfy us.

Have you ever found yourself feeling unsatisfied with your life? It's easy to become unsatisfied in our job, marriage, finances, looks, etc. This Scripture reminds us to start each morning seeking God and His love, which is the only thing that can truly satisfy our unsatisfied hearts.

Second, true joy is found in a satisfied heart.

Notice the phrase "so we may." We must seek God and His "never changing and always enough love," so we may have joy everlasting. It even says we will "sing for joy." Our hearts will be so full of love and joy that we will want to sing!

All of this is ours with only one step needed from us – seek Him each morning. I believe there is great wisdom in Moses' prayer. He knows that we must seek God as soon as we wake up. It is easy to let other things or people get in the way of our quiet time with the Lord. Before we know it, our day is spiraling out of control and our thought life is an unholy mess. This is because we did not go to the One Who Satisfies first. We might have had a full cup of coffee, but we forgot to get our spiritual cup filled.

If you find yourself in a place of dissatisfaction with your life and lacking true joy, run to the Father and seek His unfailing love. He longs to lavish it on you. His love will never change and it will always be enough.

Lord,
Thank You that Your love is unfailing! Please help me seek You faithfully every morning and allow You to fill my spiritual cup with all that I need to be truly satisfied. Increase my joy in You, Lord. Help me shine Your light to those around me so they will want to know You.
Amen.

Seeking Jehovah!

Seek ye Jehovah and his strength; Seek his face evermore.
1 Chronicles 16:11

I recently had a conversation with a dear friend who shared with me how exhausted she felt. She has an awful lot on her plate and she admitted that it was hard for her to find time to seek God's face and hear His voice in the middle of all the chaos around her.

I encouraged her to MAKE time to seek God's strength to handle all that she was dealing with and to ask for His wisdom as to what she needed to let go of. Some of the responsibilities she had taken on were making her feel overwhelmed. After some discussion, she admitted that maybe God wasn't the one compelling her to take on all that she had, but rather it was her need to feel in control. OH, HOW I CAN RELATE!

As women, we tend to think we need to take care of everything and everyone and say "yes" to every opportunity to serve that comes our way. I know it may be hard to believe, but it is possible that there are other people God has called to do something and we are in the way!

If you are feeling tired, weary or overwhelmed, take some time to seek God's face and ask for His strength to accomplish what – and only what – He has asked you to do. As He leads you, learn to let go of what is not your responsibility.

Lord,

Thank You for inviting me to seek Your face. Thank You for Your promise that if I seek You, I will find You. Thank You for giving me Your strength to do what You have called me to do. Please help me discern the difference between what I am called by You to do and what my need to control or please others compels me to do.
Amen.

Seek Strength

Seek the Lord and His strength; Seek His face continually. Psalm 105:4

"Baby, I know you are exhausted." These were the compassionate words my husband said to me as we headed into the house. (Moving takes a lot out of you!)

I thought about what Mark said as I was getting ready for bed. The thought came to me that even though I needed to take some Advil for my aching muscles, I was actually not doing too bad considering I had worked all day at my salon and then we loaded and unloaded many boxes from our current home to the new home. While I was tired, I knew that only God could be giving me the strength to do all that I had done today.

Life is like that sometimes. We go through the motions doing what has to be done, and while we might be physically, mentally, emotionally and spiritually exhausted, God gives us the strength to carry on.

In this passage, did you notice that there is an action on our part which is required in order to receive this God-given strength? We must seek the Lord – seek His face – seek His presence in our circumstances. It doesn't stop there. How often are we to seek Him? His Word says, "continually – without ceasing." This means we are to be ever mindful of the Lord – not just when things are bad or we are in crisis mode.

Being aware of God's presence and direction in our lives as we go about our day keeps us spiritually strong - which makes us able to handle whatever life throws at us. God knows what we are going to face each day. Going through a day without seeking the Lord is like not eating and trying to run a marathon. How ridiculous to think we can handle life without the strength of the One who created it!

As you go about this day – and every day – remember to seek the Lord continually so that you will have the strength that is needed to handle whatever comes.

Lord,
Thank You for Your strength! Please help me to seek You first, and may I always be mindful of my continual need for Your presence in my life. Amen.

Our Daily Bread

Give us each day our daily bread. Luke 11:3

We may have heard and recited these words a thousand times, but have we ever stopped to think about what they really mean?

When Jesus was speaking these words, it is thought by most theologians that He was speaking in Aramaic. The literal meaning for the word daily in Aramaic is "super-substantial." This leads us to interpret the verse much differently than just literally talking about food. Substantial is defined in Webster's Dictionary as "significantly great; ample."

Jesus is telling us to seek from our Heavenly Father the supernatural, substantial, (significantly great; ample) spiritual strength we need every day. Without it, we are not spiritually prepared for what we will encounter or endure. We are in spiritual warfare every day and the enemy is looking for those who are not prepared. That is no different than going into battle without a weapon!

As you prepare for your day today you will most likely shower, dress for the weather, eat breakfast, check news, email, etc. Yet, the most important thing for us to do is spiritually prepare for this day. Take the time this morning to ask the Lord for His "super-substantial" provision. If this has not been part of your regular morning routine, take the Lord at His word and see what a difference it will make.

Lord,

May I come to You every day to receive the daily bread that I need. Amen.

The Pursuit of Holiness

But just as He who called you is Holy, so be holy in all you do.
1 Peter 1:15

We tend to equate a life that is Holy to a life that is perfect. Therefore, we think being Holy in all we do is impossible. **According to Webster's Dictionary the word Holy means: Christ-like; set apart for the service and worship of God; spiritually whole or sound.**

If we have accepted Christ as our Savior and Lord then we should be pursuing a life that reflects Christ. We should be becoming "like Christ." When others look at us they should see a life that represents the One we say we belong to.

However, until we reach Heaven, we will always have a sin nature that we struggle with. We will not be able to be perfect as Christ is perfect. Praise be to God for His grace and mercy through Jesus Christ! Fortunately, it is not in our own power that we seek to live a holy life. Philippians 2:13 tells us that the Holy Spirit works in us to desire to do God's will and He gives us the power to accomplish it. It is simply up to us to surrender to the process of God changing our desires to match His and giving us the power to live it out.

As we ponder the call to live a life that is Holy, let's remember we don't do this in our own power. Let us, through the transforming power of the Holy Spirit, pursue a life that is reflective of the One we worship and serve.

Lord,

Thank You that we don't have to try to live a Holy life in our own power.
Help us to allow You to transform us into Your reflection.
Amen.

God is Great!

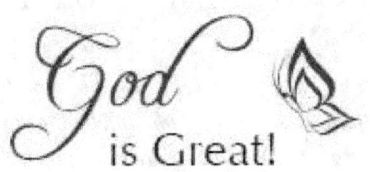

We should live like it!

God's Mighty Power

I also pray that you will understand the incredible greatness of God's power for us who believe him. This is the same mighty power that raised Christ from the dead and seated him in the place of honor at God's right hand in the heavenly realms. Ephesians 1:19-20

The power that raised Jesus from the dead is the same power that drew us to faith in Him, and it is that same power that is at work in us today. Why then do we often walk around feeling powerless in life's circumstances?

If we could honestly lay hold of the understanding that we are NOT powerless as we face anything this life throws at us, then we would have accomplished a great feat. The feelings of doom and gloom are so easy for us to gravitate to when things are not going as we would like. We walk around with that look of defeat. Let me ask you a question: Who is going to be drawn to faith in Christ by a face and an attitude like that?!

We should be living a life that screams "VICTORY!" We come to church and sing about it, listen to it, say we believe it, and then seem to forget all about it when Monday comes.

This week, I have been reminded by the Lord just how GREAT HE IS! We serve a MIGHTY, MIGHTY GOD! As Christians, we need to show the world how great He is by living like it!

Lord,

Thank You for being such a MIGHTY GOD! Please forgive me for the times I have failed to remember just how Mighty and Powerful You are! I trust You, and I want the world to see how much I love You. Help me to live a life that has VICTORIOUS written all over it!
Amen.

Thankfulness

Let us come before Him
with thanksgiving!

Thank You, Lord!

Let us come before Him with thanksgiving! Thank You, Lord! Let us come before him with thanksgiving and extol him with music and song. Psalm 95:2

Shout joyfully to the Lord, all the earth. Serve the Lord with gladness; Come before Him with joyful singing. Know that the Lord Himself is God; It is He who has made us, and not we ourselves; We are His people and the sheep of His pasture. Enter His gates with thanksgiving and His courts with praise. Give thanks to Him, bless His name. For the Lord is good; His lovingkindness is everlasting and His faithfulness to all generations. Psalm 100

This week I have been thinking about all the blessings the Lord has given me and how grateful I am for each one. They are too many to count! The greatest and most important is the gift of Salvation! We should be thankful to God for just being God, not because He gives us anything. The blessings He bestows on us are wonderful, but He deserves our thanks regardless of His gifts to us.

No matter the circumstances in our lives, we are exhorted to praise the Lord and give Him the glory He is due. A pastor once asked how much we thought it would change our lives if we spent all our time in prayer for the next thirty days just praising and thanking God. No requests – just thankfulness.

Wouldn't it be something if each day we took the time to reflect on and thank God for all He has done for us? Instead of keeping only a prayer list, what if we kept a praise list? Then we could go back and see all the praises of thanksgiving when we are feeling down. Let me encourage you today to think on all the things you are thankful for. The Lord deserves to hear it.

Lord,
THANK YOU!
AMEN!

Needs vs. Wants

And this same God who takes care of me will supply all your needs from his glorious riches, which have been given to us in Christ Jesus.
Philippians 4:19

Needs vs. Wants. That is the issue. We think we need many things that are really wants.

Frequently I hear, "I need…" from my teenage granddaughter. I usually listen and then say, "That would be a want, not a need. Let's deal with the needs first."

It can get a little irritating when our children ask for one thing after another. It feels as though the things we are providing aren't noticed or appreciated, and we are being treated like Santa Clause.

As I kissed my granddaughter goodnight recently, I told her that she needed to be thankful for all the blessings she has and that it was important to thank God for all that He's done and provided for her. I explained that it was important to have an attitude of gratitude instead of a sense of entitlement.

This made me think about how we treat God. Do we realize all that God has done for us? Do we live a life of gratitude and remember to thank God for all that He has provided for us? I fear we spend way too much time asking for things and too little time saying, "Thank You!"

In this verse we are reminded of two important facts. First, Salvation through Christ Jesus is our greatest gift from God. Second, without Christ we would not have access to God's glorious riches.

God has supplied ALL our NEEDS! Our greatest need was supplied when Christ died for us! That alone is enough! And yet…He continues to give us more than we could ask or imagine. (Ephesians 3:20)

What a great God we serve! He deserves our gratitude for all He has done for us!

Lord,
You are a Mighty, Mighty God! I love You and I Praise You! I thank You for all You have done for me! I especially thank You for the gift of Salvation through, Christ Jesus! You are a loving and merciful God! Amen!

Wisdom

If any of you lack wisdom,
you should ask for it.

Wisdom and Understanding

My son, if you accept my words and store up my commands within you, turning your ear to wisdom and applying your heart to understanding—indeed, if you call out for insight and cry aloud for understanding, and if you look for it as for silver and search for it as for hidden treasure, then you will understand the fear of the Lord and find the knowledge of God. For the Lord gives wisdom; from his mouth come knowledge and understanding. Proverbs 2:1-6

Trust in the Lord with all your heart and lean not on your own understanding; in all your ways submit to him, and he will make your paths straight. Proverbs 3:5-6

If any of you lacks wisdom, you should ask God, who gives generously to all without finding fault, and it will be given to you. James 1:5

How do you discern if it is God leading you to do something or if it is your own desires? This was the question a friend and I were discussing.

There are some things in life that are what we call "no brainers." Common sense, and a basic understanding of right and wrong, make most decisions relatively easy to make. It is when there are options placed in front of us and we are unsure which way to go, or what to do next, that can often present a challenge. This is true in small and big issues of life.

If there is one thing I have learned over the past few years, it is that I cannot lean on my own understanding in a given situation. I must seek God's wise counsel. Scripture makes it clear how we do that.

In Proverbs 2, we are instructed to: (1) know God's Word; (2) listen for God's instruction; (3) call out to God for understanding; and (4) search for it as a treasure until we find it. Are we reading God's Word, listening and calling out to God in prayer, and waiting until we are sure before we move forward?

I find that all too often I am quick to act and slow to understand. I want things done yesterday! I can get impatient and God has to remind me that I am on His time table – He is not on mine.

Are you facing a situation or decision in which you are really not sure exactly what to do? Don't make the mistake of listening to your human understanding, but seek God's wisdom and direction. In James we are promised that if we lack wisdom, we must ask for it, in faith, and it will be given. Let's take God at His word.

Lord,
Please give me ears to hear and a mind to comprehend what You are directing me to do in every situation I face. Help me to be patient and to understand that Your ways are higher than my ways. Please give me the wisdom I need to discern Your will from my own, and the desire to be obedient to Your will once it is revealed to me.
Amen

Integrity

He grants a treasure of common sense to the honest. He is a shield to those who walk with integrity. Proverbs 2:7

The second chapter of Proverbs gives us wonderful instruction on the benefits of wisdom. Verse 7 really caught my eye. It says that the Lord gives common sense to the honest. Let's think about this for a minute. Common sense is another phrase for wisdom. One of the definitions in Webster's for the word honest was full of truth. How are we to be filled with truth?

We know that Jesus is The Way, The Truth and The Life, so we know that we must first have accepted Christ as Savior to be full of Truth. However, we must also read His Word and be in communication with Him in order to recognize truth from a lie. Therefore, in order to have wisdom, we must be full of the truth of God's Word.

Have you ever thought, "What has happened to integrity?" The Webster's Dictionary defines integrity as moral soundness.

The second part of this verse says that the Lord is a shield to those who walk with integrity. In Ephesians we are told to put on the shield of faith in order to extinguish the flaming arrows of the evil one. OK – follow me here – if the evil one is looking for whom he may devour, then he is looking for those who are not walking in their faith – not trusting God above themselves or others. He is looking for the ones who are vulnerable!

The evil one wants to destroy the moral soundness of Christians, so we will be ineffective witnesses for Christ. In order to stand against the enemy's attacks on our integrity, (moral soundness) we must put on the shield of faith in Christ. We must choose Christ when we are tempted to act against God's moral instruction.

One of the many lessons I learned from my parents was how important it is to have integrity. From the time I was very young, I remember people saying how they admired my father's integrity. I am proud to be my father's daughter and bear his good name. My mother used to say, "Remember who you are and Whose you are." I don't just bear the name of my earthly father – I bear the name of my Heavenly Father. The question is, do I live like it? Do I live my life worthy of the name I bear?

Now let's put it all together. God grants a treasure of wisdom to those who are full of His Word and He is a shield against the enemy for those who walk in moral soundness. If you want to have good common sense – read God's Word. If you want to have good moral character – then choose to trust God above all else. THE END!

Lord,
Please help me to stay in Your word and in communication with You, so that I will know Your will and act accordingly.
Amen.

Humility

We all have sinned.

All Have Sinned

For all have sinned and fall short of the glory of God. Romans 3:23

Brothers and sisters, if someone is caught in a sin, you who live by the Spirit should restore that person gently. But watch yourselves, or you also may be tempted. Carry each other's burdens, and in this way you will fulfill the law of Christ. If anyone thinks they are something when they are not, they deceive themselves. Galatians 6:1-3

Which one are you? The one caught up in sin, the one sent to help restore, or the one that thinks they are something when they are not?

If we are honest, each of us has probably been all three at different times in our lives. It is so easy to get swept up in sin if we are not careful. It is heartbreaking to watch it happen to a friend, but it is extremely easy to let that lead to a judgmental spirit.

I have heard different teachings on this passage, and I have a different way of looking at it than some. I agree that if you keep company with those who are caught up in sin, it may be easy for you to fall into the same sin. However, I have another thought on this verse.

Right after we are instructed to help restore our brother or sister, we are warned to watch ourselves so that we may not be tempted. Tempted to do what? It goes on to say that while we are to help carry each other's burdens, we should be careful to not think too highly of ourselves.

I think Paul is making the point that not only can we fall into the same sin, but rather some of us may fall into the sin of pride. It is easy for us to feel better about ourselves if we can find fault in someone else. I have found this to be especially true when we don't want to hear what the Lord is trying to say to us about the condition of our lives.

We all sin and fall short of the glory of God. Let's not think we're something when we're not. We are redeemed because we needed redeeming by the Redeemer – Amen?

As you examine your life today, allow God to speak to you about the areas of sin that need to be surrendered to Him. Let's be careful not to judge others caught up in sin because in doing so, we have just sinned.

Lord,
Thank You for being my Redeemer! Thank You that I no longer have to live under the oppression of sin! Help me to not fall into the trap of thinking that I am better than someone else as I see them struggling. As You lead me, help me to be loving and honest, as I encourage them to get back into a right relationship with You.
Amen.

Forgive

Forgive as you have been forgiven.

Forgive, as You Have Been Forgiven

This, then, is how you should pray. Our Father in heaven, hallowed be your name, your kingdom come, your will be done, on earth as it is in heaven. Give us today our daily bread. And forgive us our debts, as we also have forgiven our debtors. And lead us not into temptation, but deliver us from the evil one. Matthew 6:9-13

While reading this passage in Matthew, it struck me a little differently than it had before. I have heard and recited the Lord's Prayer more times than I can count. However, the line about forgiveness stood out to me.

Maybe it was because I had recently been offended by something someone did and said. They didn't set out to hurt me or offend me, and yet their insensitivity hit me rather hard. I wanted to cry, and I felt justified in my anger towards them. Then I heard the still small voice of my Savior speak to my heart. "Lynn, I want you to forgive." Honestly, Lord, I think they need to know just how badly they hurt me, and … "Lynn, I want you to forgive them, just like I have forgiven you." Ouch! There is was. I was hit right between the eyes with truth.

There are more sins I have, and will, commit in my lifetime than I will ever know or be able to count. Yet, Christ died and shed His innocent blood to pay for my sin. I am forgiven! How then, do I have the right to hold on to an offense?

This doesn't mean that my feelings didn't get hurt or that what the other person did and said wasn't offensive or insensitive. It simply means that I should take my hurt to the

Lord and ask Him to help me forgive them. Being reminded of how much He has forgiven me, makes it a little easier.

The Lord has shown great mercy to us. How can we justify holding back mercy from someone else?

Lord,
Thank You for Your forgiveness! Please help me to forgive others as You have forgiven me.
Amen.

Friendship

Iron sharpens Iron

A Good Friend

As iron sharpens iron, so a friend sharpens a friend. Proverbs 27:17

Do you have that one friend who will tell you the truth, even if it's not what you want to hear? Do you have a prayer and/ or accountability partner?

Along my faith journey, the Lord has placed several of these people in my life. I need them! These people have helped to shape my Christian faith. They've helped bring me closer to the knowledge and understanding of God's Word and His love for me. Their prayers of intercession have been used by God to bring healing into my life. The godly advice they have given me has held me accountable to live out what I claim to believe.

We all need godly friends. Are you surrounding yourself with people who tell you what you want to hear or people who tell you what you need to hear? It is easy to find those who will agree with you, but difficult to find a friend who will speak truth in love, even if it hurts.

Here's another question – what kind of friend are you? Do you agree with your friends even when you know they're wrong? Do you shy away from being truthful because you fear they might reject you? God's Word tells us that we are to sharpen each other as friends.

Let's look at these next two verses. *For the word of God is alive and powerful. It is sharper than the sharpest two-edged sword, cutting between soul and spirit, between joint and marrow. It exposes our innermost thoughts and desires.* Hebrews 4:12
Put on salvation as your helmet, and take the sword of the Spirit, which is the word of God. Ephesians 6:17

Notice something here? The word of God is sharper than any sword and our only defensive weapon against the enemy. Therefore, if we are called as friends to sharpen each other – what do we do that with? The word of God! We should speak truth and life into each other through the Word of God.

If you do not currently have a friend who is lovingly speaking God's truth into your life, holding you accountable and praying for you, then maybe you need to evaluate your friendships. Are you the kind of friend YOU would want? Are you willing to be a godly friend to someone else?

Let's allow God to take full inventory of the friends we spend time with and listen to. May we also be the kind of friend that God calls us to be. We need to be willing to be sharpened and to sharpen.

Lord,
Thank You for being the greatest Friend I could ever have! You laid down Your life so I could live. Help me be the kind of friend that speaks Your word of truth and life into others. May I also be willing to receive it from the godly friends you have placed in my life. Thank You for ALL You have done for me and for giving me wonderful friends!
Amen.

Worry

Restless and Distracted

Distractions of Life

Give heed to me and answer me; I am restless in my complaint and am surely distracted. Psalm 55:2

But Martha was distracted with much serving. And she went up to him and said, "Lord, do you not care that my sister has left me to serve alone? Tell her then to help me." Luke 10:40

My heart went out to a friend who was carrying some very heavy burdens on her shoulders. She said, "I am very distracted right now." I have known that feeling all too well. The Lord has spoken to my heart again and again on this issue, and I am a slow learner!

It is easy to get weighed down by all the distractions of life. Some are big and some are rather small. No matter the size, they equally distract us from the place of peace and rest.

Look at Psalm 55:2. David says he is restless and distracted. I dare say one does not come without the other. David is doing exactly what he needs to do. He takes his need to the Lord.

The same thing is happening in Luke 10:40. Martha is "distracted with much serving." Now I know there are some tired women out there saying, "Me too!" Martha was all upset because Mary wouldn't help with the dinner preparation. What does she do? She tattles on Mary to Jesus! Have you ever tattled on someone to the Lord? I have! We are serving and serving and all out of sorts because… we need help and no one will help… and if we don't do it then… it just won't get done and… we can't have that!! Sound familiar?

One commentary said Martha was, "drawn off" from hearing the word because she was "drawn to" much serving. This was an opportunity for Martha to sit at the Lord's feet and let Him feed her, and instead, she was consumed with feeding Him. Maybe I am going out on a limb here, but if Martha had decided to sit a spell, what do you think would have happened? Don't you think if Jesus can turn water into wine, heal the sick, feed the 5,000, and raise the dead, He could figure out something for dinner?!

I am such a Martha sometimes! I think I have to do it all myself. I forget that I serve a Mighty, Mighty, God! If he can fling the stars in space, He can take care of my needs far better than I can! My challenge is to bring my needs and burdens to Him, lay them at His feet, and in faith –LEAVE THEM THERE!

No matter what you are carrying today, big or small, God knows exactly what you need, and He will provide it, in His timing, and in His way. He asks us to trust Him. Sometimes I think He waits until there can be no doubt as to Who was responsible for the provision and/or deliverance, so we don't get too self-reliant. Let's take the time to sit a while, and cry out to the Lord. Ask for His provision. Let's keep our eyes fixed on Him, instead of the distraction, and wait patiently for Him to act.

Lord,

Thank You that we can come to You with our burdens and distractions of life! We ask now, Father that You would provide what we need. Help us to have faith as we wait patiently for You to act.
Amen.

Dedicated to the Lord

Now I'm dedicating him to the Lord, and as long as he lives, he will be dedicated to the Lord. 1 Samuel 1:28

"How are you doing?" I asked. As tears began to well up in my friend's eyes, she replied, "It's really hard." Her baby was now eighteen and heading off to college the next day. She was sending her daughter out into the big world and it was a little unnerving.

As I thought about what my friend was going through, I remembered the story of Hannah. After years of struggling with infertility, Hannah begged God to give her a son, promising to dedicate him to the Lord's service. The Lord answered her request. She had a son and named him Samuel, which means, "God has heard."

When Samuel was about three years old, Hannah took him to the Tabernacle in Shiloh, and placed him under the care and tutelage of Eli, the priest. Today, this would have been a lot like sending him off to a Christian boarding school. Hannah and her husband lived in Ramah, approximately fifteen miles from Shiloh. We are told that Hannah visited Samuel often and made him a new robe each year. I am sure that Hannah's heart ached from missing her son between visits. I imagine those were the longest fifteen miles of her life, every time she traveled back home. However, Hannah knew that God had given her this son, to be dedicated back to Him, so he could be used by Him. Hannah was faithful to God with what had faithfully been given to her. What a powerful testimony!

We are raising our granddaughter and she is in the first year of high school. There have been many days that I have worried about her. One particular day, I was consumed with worry. Then, I heard the still small voice of my Heavenly Father, "Lynn, dedicate her to My care." I suddenly realized, it is my job to pray for, love, encourage, and guide her, but I must let her grow up, and let God be God in her life.

No matter what stage of life you are in – from becoming a parent, to watching your children become parents – remember that we are asked to dedicate our children back to God. He loves them more than we ever could, and He has a plan for each of them.

Lord,
Help me to remember that my child is on loan from You. They are Your gifts to me, and I dedicate them back to You. Please watch over them, protect them from the evil one, and help them to follow You. Give me wisdom, strength and peace, as I go through each stage of life with them. As they enter adulthood, help me to let go and allow them to become all that You have created them to be.
Amen.

Rest

Come with Me
and rest.

Rest and Relaxation!

The apostles gathered around Jesus and reported to him all they had done and taught. Then, because so many people were coming and going that they did not even have a chance to eat, he said to them, "Come with Me by yourselves to a quiet place and get some rest." Mark 6:30-31

Then Jesus said, "Come to me, all who are weary and carry heavy burdens, and I will give you rest." Matthew 11:28

After the disciples had been all consumed with teaching and ministering to people after the feeding of the 5,000, Jesus invites them to rest. They hadn't even taken time to eat! Have you ever been so busy you forgot to eat a meal?

When my granddaughter was little, I told her she needed to have some quiet time. (Mostly, I needed it!) I put her in our office on the sofa with some books and a blanket and told her to take a time-out from running around and just rest for a bit. Sometimes I wish someone would tell me to go take a "time-out!"

We need a moment to sit and think about things. To just stop for a minute and calm down – take a breath. I want to encourage you to take a "time-out." You may not be able to get away for a weekend, but try to find some time to just rest and relax for a while.

Jesus got in a boat and took a nap during a storm! I think He was making a point – don't you? Sometimes we just need a nap! Amen?

Are you carrying some heavy burdens? Are you feeling weary? Christ calls us to come to Him, and He promises us that

He will give us rest. Listen to the still small voice of your Savior giving you permission to rest – to take a time-out – to come away with Him for a while. You will be so glad you did!

Lord,
Thank You so much for times of rest and renewal!
Amen!

Watching and Waiting

Blessed are those who listen to me, watching daily at my doors, waiting at my doorway. Proverbs 8:34

Many things and people compete for our time and attention. We often feel guilty in this day and time if we are not busy doing something.

This verse is another reminder that we are blessed when we listen, watch and wait. This often requires quietness and stillness. I am working on this – or rather the Lord is working on me concerning this.

I am trying to quiet the noise around me. I am currently working on not having the TV on in the background, no radio on the way to work and back, not talking on my phone as much, being careful to listen more and talk less. I believe if I can do these things, I will be amazed at how it will change my life.

I encourage you to take this journey with me. Cut out the noise as much as you can. Ask the Lord to speak to you and see what happens.

Lord,
Please help me listen, watch and wait in quietness.
Amen.

He Sustains Me!

I lie down and sleep; I wake again, because the Lord sustains me.
Psalm 3:5

Has worry over the circumstances of life ever stolen your sleep? There is nothing worse than a night with very little to any sleep. You are drained and tired and barely making it through the day. Too many of these nights can easily affect your health.

I found myself recently in need of some good sleep. I came across this verse. Coincidence? I think not.

When we face trying times, we need our rest in order to handle the adversity with all the mental, physical, emotional and spiritual strength possible. Rest is crucial to our earthly bodies.

In this passage, David is fearful of being pursued and overtaken by his enemies. However, he needed to rest – to sleep. The Lord gave him full confidence to lay his worries and fears at His feet and rest. David says that he was able to do this because of the sustaining power of the Lord.

This was the part that grabbed my attention. To what or to whom do we turn for comfort in difficult times? Is it someone we love or something that makes us feel better for a moment?

Sustain means "to provide what is needed for someone to exist." (Webster's Online dictionary) I don't know about you, but there is only one name that comes to mind who fits that bill – Jesus! I am not going to be able to get what I need to exist from any other source! So, why is it we spend so much time looking for it everywhere else?!

Maybe you are like me and worry can grab hold of you and keep you up at night. Where we must run is into the arms of our Dear Savior and rest – sleep – and be sustained.

Lord,
Thank You for sustaining me! Please help me to always run to you for all that I need rather than someone else or something else. You are my Rock, my Fortress and my Strong Tower! It is in You that I find my strength! Please give me sweet sleep and help me face another day in Your sustaining power!
Amen.

Encouragement

Press on and
don't give up.

Press On

Not that I have already obtained all this, or have already arrived at my goal, but I press on to take hold of that for which Christ Jesus took hold of me. Brothers and sisters, I do not consider myself yet to have taken hold of it. But one thing I do: Forgetting what is behind and straining toward what is ahead, I press on toward the goal to win the prize for which God has called me heavenward in Christ Jesus. Philippians 3:12-14

In this passage, Paul is encouraging the Philippians to "press on." I think we all need someone in our cheering section saying, "Keep going! You can do it! Don't quit!" If we take the time to listen, I believe we can hear those words coming from our Heavenly Father.

It's easy to give up when life gets tough or we think we have messed up. God's Word instructs us to forget the former things and keep pressing on toward the final goal – Heaven with Christ Jesus!

There is so much meat in this passage and we could spend days dissecting each point. However, what I want to encourage you to lay hold of is that no matter where you are in your race and no matter how hard it gets, keep going. Don't give up! Forget the past and press on. With the Lord's help, you can do it.

Lord Jesus,
Thank You so much for helping me to press on and continue the race! Help me to apprehend all that my human mind can comprehend until I reach the final goal of seeing you face to face in Heaven! Amen.

All Will Become Clear

When I was a child, I used to speak like a child, think like a child, reason like a child; when I became a man, I did away with childish things. For now we see in a mirror dimly, but then face to face; now I know in part, but then I will know fully just as I also have been fully known.
1 Corinthians 13:11-12

"Sometimes I wish I was still five and didn't know all the stuff I now know." These were the words my granddaughter said to me. I knew exactly what she was saying. Unfortunately, she had to grow up too fast, and it was easier when she didn't know and understand the world quite so much.

However, I pointed out to her that with knowledge also come blessings. She has accepted Christ and understands what it means to have a relationship with Him. She also has many privileges that being older brings. While there is an innocence that is lost, there is also an understanding and an experiencing of deeper things as well.

In this passage, Paul makes the comparison that just like our childhood knowledge limited us in our understanding, we are also limited in our true understanding of our Heavenly Father this side of Heaven.

We can't possibly know and understand all that will be revealed to us one day in Glory. As children we had to depend on others to teach and guide us with a blind trust. We are much like that as believers. We don't always understand what God is doing in our lives, but we must trust as children do, until one day we see clearly. When that day comes, I am confident that many of us will be very surprised by how much we thought we knew! Until then, we must press on and look for God's hand in our life – even if the understanding is not fully there – we must strive to trust and follow.

Lord,
I look forward to the day when I will fully understand and know. It is hard to imagine what it will be like to see You face to face. Oh, how I look forward to that day! Until that time, Lord, help me to know You, trust You and follow You, even if the way seems unclear.
Amen.

Follow Me

Then Jesus said to his disciples, "Whoever wants to be my disciple must deny themselves and take up their cross and follow me. Matthew 16:24

"No one ever said this was going to be easy, Lynn. God may be taking you to places you do not want to go, but you must follow Him and do what He leads you to do." These were the words one of my precious friends texted me. She had no idea how much I needed to read them.

Facing some very challenging circumstances caused me to think twice about pressing on and the desire to give up was creeping in. After I read my friend's text, I realized that it addressed one of the deep thoughts I have been struggling with for over a year. Sometimes, I really don't want to do what God is asking me to do because it seems too hard, scary or overwhelming. There is often deep struggle within me. Truly, I desire to do God's will and yet I sometimes struggle to be obedient when it gets uncomfortable. Here's a newsflash – God did not call me to be comfortable! He called me to trust and obey.

This verse makes me think about how much it cost my Savior to take up His cross – which He did not deserve – and be obedient to God unto death. Christ allowed men to beat Him, spit on Him, place a crown of thorns on His head, and drive large painful nails into His hands and feet. Worst of all, He became sin when He knew no sin, in order that I might live. Why then do I want to give up so easily when life gets hard or messy?!

A few years ago, my father made a statement that had a huge impact on me. He said, "We want all the blessings of being a follower of Christ without any sacrifice." He is right. We desire "Easy Street." Don't mess up our nest!

Christ tells us that if we want to be His disciple, we must deny ourselves. What does that mean? It means that we can't be consumed with our comfort level. Carrying a cross is not comfortable. It will be challenging and difficult at times. However, we must remember that we do not carry that cross in our own strength. Our Savior is leading, protecting and supplying the strength we need to do what He has asked of us. It is when we try to do it in our own power or with resistance that we find ourselves weakened by the load.

So, my friend, is God asking you to follow Him into some challenging and unfamiliar territory? Many circumstances of life often seem that way. Do not fear – He is with you! His plans are for your good and His glory. Don't give up! Take up your cross and follow Him!

Lord,
Please help me to follow You wherever You lead me.
Amen

Calling

So do not be ashamed of the testimony about our Lord or of me his prisoner. Rather, join with me in suffering for the gospel, by the power of God. He has saved us and called us to a holy life— not because of anything we have done but because of his own purpose and grace. This grace was given us in Christ Jesus before the beginning of time, but it has now been revealed through the appearing of our Savior, Christ Jesus, who has destroyed death and has brought life and immortality to light through the gospel. And of this gospel I was appointed a herald and an apostle and a teacher. That is why I am suffering as I am. Yet this is no cause for shame, because I know whom I have believed, and am convinced that he is able to guard what I have entrusted to him until that day. 2 Timothy 1:8-12

According to Webster's dictionary, calling means, the action of one who calls; an inner urging toward some profession or activity; one's occupation, profession, or trade; vocation.

The Lord is the one who calls. He is the one who puts the desire or *inner urging* inside of us to do what He has asked us to do. Why then is it that we are afraid to step out in faith and fulfill the call? Are we afraid we will fail, be laughed at, or that we will have to pay too high a price?

The truth is we will not fail if we keep our eyes on Christ and not on our own strength. We may be laughed at by others, even our own family and friends. That certainly happened to Jesus, but praise God, He didn't let that keep Him from fulfilling His calling!

We may have to pay a price we don't want to pay, but as the Scripture tells us in Philippians 4:19 **"… Nothing**

compares to the glorious riches in Christ Jesus." Our reward is in Heaven, not here on earth. Christ paid the highest price of all, and aren't we glad He did?!

If the Lord is calling you, and He has put an urging in your heart toward a particular task, He will give you the power to accomplish it! Step out! He's waiting…

Lord,
Give us the strength to respond to Your calling on our lives. May we be a light to lead others to You. May we not be ashamed of the Gospel of Jesus Christ or live in fear of what others will say about us. Free us from the worry of failing or being rejected by others. Help us to keep our eyes fixed on You, and You alone.
Amen.

Guidance

Your steps are
made secure.

Steps Secured

The Lord directs the steps of the godly. He delights in every detail of their lives. Psalm 37:23

The steps of a man are established by the Lord; And He delights in his way. Psalm 37:23

Established means, settled securely and unconditionally.

    The steps of a man are settled securely and unconditionally. This means that the Lord makes secure the steps of His children and He does this unconditionally. It is not based on us living a sinless life. We make mistakes, we stumble, we slip, and the enemy tries to tempt us to get off track. However, we are more richly blessed by the Lord when we follow in the direction He is leading us.
    Times of trial, difficulty, and even failure can be used by the Lord to bring us to a place of deeper dependence on Him.

Thy word is a light unto my path and a lamp unto my feet. Psalm 119:105

    This verse reminds us that the Lord typically shows us one simple step at a time – not ten miles down the road. He asks solely for our obedience, which leads us to a life surrendered to Him and rich in faith and trust.
    Delights means, to take pleasure in.

I don't know about you, but I find the thought that the Lord takes pleasure in every detail of my life both overwhelming and extremely comforting. I am a detail person, but I don't always delight or take pleasure in having to handle all of the details that I have to handle on a daily basis. Yet, my Heavenly Father takes pleasure in seeing to every detail of my life! WOW!

Let's not leave this passage without acknowledging one huge truth. When left up to our own power we can only do so much, but when what we are doing is in and through God's power we can accomplish infinitely more! HE orders our steps! HE sets our steps securely! The Creator of everything that has ever existed is the one who directs and secures my steps! When God is for us then who can be against us?!

So my challenge to us today is to commit to walk in the way God desires for us, completely surrendered and dependent on Him. We should be confident in the promise that He has set securely and unconditionally our steps. If we allow Him to direct us and not resist Him, we can accomplish (through His power) more than we could ever imagine. Remember, God Almighty takes pleasure in every detail of our lives!

Lord,
Please make my steps be the steps You would have me take. Set my feet secure! Thank You for seeing to every detail of my life! Help me to trust You with even the smallest detail.
Amen.

Go to the High Places

He maketh my feet like hinds feet: And setteth me upon my high places.
Psalm 18:33

Over my lifetime I have heard and read this verse several times. It appears three times in Scripture. (The two other references are, 2 Samuel 22:34 and Habakkuk 3:19.)

The other day a friend and I were having a discussion about this verse and its meaning. I went home that day and did a little digging.

Did you know that the Hind is a female red deer who lives only in the mountain regions? The rear feet of the Hind deer step precisely in the same spot where the front feet have just been. Every step of the Hind is meticulously planned and focused, making it the most surefooted of all mountain animals.

This information made this verse come alive to me! Did you notice this is a female deer? I love that! Ladies, I see this verse as a promise!

If we are willing to surrender to the will of God and the power of the Holy Spirit, we will be made strong and surefooted to be able to maneuver through the rough and rocky terrain of this life.

Look at the last part of this verse. It reads, "And setteth me upon my high places." What do you think that means? It means that there is a high place that God has just for you!

The rocky mountainous terrain of this life is for a purpose. It creates opportunity for us to learn to depend on the Lord in every step we take. This is the way we grow closer to Him and stronger in Him. Then we can experience Him, and be used by Him, in ways we never imagined!

Sometimes, the safety of the low places seems easier. Going to the high places appears hard and difficult. We like the easy, carefree path. Our Savior is calling us to go to the High Places with Him. He tells us where to step and He makes our feet secure. So, let's go! We have nothing to lose but our fear and self-reliance.

Lord,
Take me to the High Places prepared just for me! Thank You for making my feet surefooted and showing me where to step! Help me to cast off fear and doubt and lead me where You want to take me.
Amen.

The *Best*  Laid Plans

This was not the plan!

The Plan

Now listen, you who say, "Today or tomorrow we will go to this or that city, spend a year there, carry on business and make money." Why, you do not even know what will happen tomorrow. What is your life? You are a mist that appears for a little while and then vanishes. Instead, you ought to say, "If it is the Lord's will, we will live and do this or that."
James 4:13-15

You can make many plans, but the LORD's purpose will prevail.
Proverbs 19:21

Do not boast about tomorrow, for you do not know what a day may bring.
Proverbs 27:1

"This was not in the plan, Lord!" These were the words I cried as I faced another major life change. I had a plan and I felt strongly that God was directing me in that plan. I thought it was His plan, and then all the sudden – out of nowhere – BOOM! Change of plans! The Lord took my toy box and turned it upside down!

Anyone who knows me knows that I am neat and organized. I like everything in its place and don't move it or I will not be able to find it later. I truly believe we are born with these types of proclivities, but I also think some of these habits are the way we try to have a sense of control.

I was forgetful as a child. If I didn't write it down or have it on a calendar, I didn't retain it. My mother taught me early in life to take responsibility for remembering important things by writing them in my school assignment book and in my pocket calendar. These are tools of survival I still use today. My mother used to say, "I think you would forget your head, if it weren't attached to your body." I think she might have been correct.

Being organized and neat is not my challenge, but the ability to let go of trying to control everything in my day and to not hyper-function, is. It was more than difficult for me to let go of my plans and willingly let God's plan unfold in my life.

Almost two years ago, Mark and I began raising our granddaughter – and people, this was not in the plan! We were working towards a three to five year plan of possibly relocating and moving closer to where our children and grandchildren all lived. We were going to buy a little town home or condo and downsize. Well, God said, "No, that's not the plan. You are going to raise your teenage granddaughter." WHAT?! NO! THAT IS NOT THE PLAN, LORD!

As the Lord is gently and lovingly leading me through this process, I have realized that His plan is really so much better than mine. There are moments I think, "I can't do this. It's too much responsibility and it is harder than I thought it would be." It is at those times, I cry out to the Lord, (and sometimes a family member or counselor). He reminds me that He is in control, this is His plan, and He will help me to accomplish it – if I will surrender it to Him. As I look back over the last couple years, I realize that each moment, good and difficult, has been worth it.

So, maybe you're a planner and you think you had it all figured out. Then suddenly, God interrupted your life with His plan. Let me encourage you today to lay hold of it. Surrender to it, and let God take you on a wonderful journey that is ultimately better than anything you could think or imagine.

Lord,
I ask you to help me accept Your plans for me and to rest in the knowledge that You are in control. I don't have to do it all in my power and it doesn't have to go my way. Thank You, for leading me every step of the way. Amen.

He's Got the Plan!

For I know the plans I have for you," declares the LORD, "plans to prosper you and not to harm you, plans to give you hope and a future.
Jeremiah 29:11

This is the verse that my granddaughter has written on her heart – as well as other places in her room – and claims as her life verse. It blesses me when I hear her reciting it to me when I start to get anxious over something. She will say, "Nana, He's got the plan!"

Recently, Mark and I have been praying about some important plans and looking for God's direction. We have claimed this scripture in those times of prayer. We love the song *Trust His Heart* by Wayne Watson and Cynthia Clawson, and Mark and I have sung it many times. The message never gets old – When you can't trace His hand, trust His heart.

Are you facing some life changes? Is there some big decision you need to make and you are looking for God's plan? May God's Word encourage you today to know that He has your best interest at heart. He has the perfect plan – even if it is not what you thought it would be. It often isn't!

We don't always see what God is doing, but we must trust the heart of our Savior and know that His plans for us are good.

Lord,
Thank You for Your provision and Your plans! Help me to trust You more each day!
Amen.

Our Mighty Warrior

Be still and know
that He is God!

Be Still and Know

God is our refuge and strength, an ever-present help in trouble. Therefore we will not fear, though the earth give way and the mountains fall into the heart of the sea, though its waters roar and foam and the mountains quake with their surging... Be still, and know that I am God...
Psalm 46:1-11

For as long as I can remember, I have read and heard verse 10 many times. However, a few years ago I read the entire eleven verses of this chapter and it made verse 10 really come alive to me.

Even though there is complete calamity all around us, in this world and often in our own lives, we are instructed to remember that: God is our help in times of trouble, we should not fear; He will sustain us, provide for us, protect us, and deliver us. We are reminded to honor the Lord for all of His provisions and we are to "Be still and know that He is God!" Psalm 46:10.

We can often allow the concerns of this life to take over our thought life and consume us with worry and fear. This scripture calls us to remember that "God is our refuge and strength, an ever-present help in times of trouble!" We are to worship Him, honor Him as our Lord and Savior, wait patiently for Him to act and know that HE IS GOD!

As women, we often feel responsible for many things in life – family, career, friendships, church ministry, etc. In a world that fights to keep us constantly busy, I pray we will make time daily to sit quietly before the Lord and experience the many blessings that it brings.

Lord,
May my daily quiet time before Your throne be a priority in my life. Please help me focus on You, rather than my circumstances. Help me to remember all Your benefits!
Amen.

Author and Perfecter

Looking unto Jesus the author and perfecter of our faith, who for the joy that was set before him endured the cross, despising its shame, and hath sat down at the right hand of the throne of God. Hebrews 12:2

Author – a person who has written something; especially: a person who has written a book or who writes many books; a person who starts or creates something (such as a plan or idea.)

Perfecter – To make perfect; Finisher – Brings to completion.

If we take these definitions and insert them into the verse, it helps us understand it a little better. Jesus created our faith and is also the One who will make it perfect and bring it to its completion. That is a lot to wrap our finite minds around!

This reminds us that He is the Alpha and the Omega, Beginning and The End! (See Revelation), The Author and Perfecter/Finisher! Nothing existed before Him and nothing exists without Him! Mind-blowing, isn't it?

I personally find it freeing! God created me to desire faith in Him. He also will perfect that faith when I see Him face to face in Heaven. Until then, He is the one who grows my faith in Him. What is my responsibility? To let Him! To get out of His way! To yield to Him! To surrender!

Lord,
Thank You for creating me to desire to know You. Thank You that You will make my faith in You complete on the day I see You face to face. I ask You to help me get out of Your way as You grow me into the woman You desire me to be.
Amen!

Thought
Life

The Battle is in the mind.

I Want to be Blessed!

Wherever you go and whatever you do, you will be blessed.
Deuteronomy 28:6

In this passage, Moses is speaking to the Israelites prior to their entering the Promised Land. He is encouraging them to remember the blessings that come from living a life of obedience to God. He instructs them to live obediently so that, wherever they go and whatever they do, they will be blessed.

When I read this I thought, I want to be blessed! The Lord spoke to my heart – "I long to pour out My blessings on my obedient children." Isn't this how we feel toward our children when we see them living obedient lives? As parents, we are much more inclined to give privileges to a respectful, obedient child rather than a disrespectful, disobedient child.

This does not mean that we must be sinless in order to receive God's blessings. That's impossible. However, it does mean that moment by moment we are to surrender our hearts and minds to be made obedient to Christ. We should make every effort to be in pursuit of obedience.

Our flesh will always be at war with the Holy Spirit within us, but we have a choice. We can allow our flesh and its worldly desires to control us OR the Holy Spirit within us to have control. God longs to bless us in ways we cannot begin to imagine, but He does not bless our disobedience.

I don't know about you, but I want all the blessings the Lord has for me! He has already blessed us with the greatest blessing of all – the gift of Salvation! He owes us NOTHING!

Yet, His Word tells us that He longs to bless us! What a great God we serve!!

Do not confuse the blessings the Lord longs to bestow on us with the popular prosperity preaching these days! We will have struggles in this life and some of the most obedient followers of Christ have known suffering. However, it is often out of our suffering that some of the greatest spiritual blessings come.

The Lord does often bless His people with financial and material blessings. Hopefully if and/or when we receive these kinds of blessings, we are good stewards and never take them for granted.

The greatest blessing we will receive from an obedient life in Christ is the sweet fellowship we have with Him. After all that He has done for us, our desire to be obedient to Him is the least we can do to show our gratitude.

Lord,
Thank You for the blessings of Salvation! Thank You for all the blessings You so freely bestow on Your people. Please help me live a life that is in obedience to You, so that I can receive all the blessings You have for me. Amen.

The Battle Begins in the Mind

So letting your sinful nature control your mind leads to death. But letting the Spirit control your mind leads to life and peace. Romans 8:6

All day long, I was angry. Throughout the day, I was consumed with thoughts of what I wanted to say to express that anger to the one who had disappointed and betrayed me. I played it over and over in my mind. By the afternoon, I was a complete bundle of nerves. Then I heard the still small voice of the Lord, "Lynn, who is in control of your mind?"

The answer was clear. My sin nature was in control of my thoughts, rather than taking my feelings to the Lord and letting Him have control. I had to be honest with God about how I was feeling and asked Him to help me see the situation through His eyes and control my anger.

I am not going to tell you that I felt immediate release of all feelings of anger, but I had made the choice to ask for the Lord's help in controlling my thoughts and actions concerning those feelings. Often, the choice comes first and the feelings follow.

The Scripture tells us that if we allow our sinful nature to control our minds, it leads to death. The only way to have life and peace is through the power of the Holy Spirit controlling our minds. We have a choice between life and death. It is my desire to surrender my mind and tell my sin nature to yield to the authority of Jesus Christ. There are days this will be a moment by moment process. However, this is the only way to have life and peace.

If you are struggling with your thought life, let me encourage you to talk to the Lord and ask Him for His help. The Scripture tells us to take every thought captive to the mind of Christ. This is a learned practice and it takes time. Don't give up! It will be worth it!

Lord,
Please continue to help me allow the Holy Spirit to have full control of my mind. For I know this is the only way for me to have life and peace. Amen.

Shame
and Guilt

He makes all things new!

It is by Grace!

And if by grace, then it cannot be based on works; if it were, grace would no longer be grace. Romans 11:6

So now there is no condemnation for those who belong to Christ Jesus. Romans 8:1

Grace – we can't earn it, we don't deserve it, we can have it if we choose it, and it's free!

"Grace, Grace, God's Grace! Grace that is greater than all our sin!" I love that hymn!

Here is my simple question for today – If we can't earn grace and it's free, then why don't we live like we have it?

We beat ourselves up, choosing to live under the oppression of guilt, shame and unforgiveness. Shame is a powerful drug. Why do I use the word "drug" when describing shame? It is because I think we can become addicted to it.

We can use shame to avoid doing what God has called us to do. We justify that there is no way God could or would possibly use us for a particular work because we have done (fill in the blank.)

Our pastor spoke Sunday on the issue of shame and guilt. It is a powerful weapon that we can use against ourselves and others. We can allow the enemy to use it against us as well. Why would we do this when Christ Jesus has set us free from condemnation? The price He paid on the cross is enough! There is no need to continue wounding ourselves and others when the wounds of Christ have healed us! By His stripes we are healed! (1 Peter 2:24)

If we could earn or work our way into Heaven, then why do we need a Savior? No need for grace at all if works take care of it – right? Faith is a complete waste of time and grace is not grace.

That's what we're saying every time we allow ourselves to go down the dark road of shame and guilt. We are basically telling Jesus that His sacrifice wasn't enough to cover our sin. How arrogant of us! Let's not confuse humility with self-deprecating behavior either. Feeling guilty isn't holy or humble. It's still all about SELF!

Please understand that when we sin, it is important to confess our sin to God and ask Him to help us turn from that sin. However, it is not right to do that and then continue to live in the land of shame. That's exactly what the enemy wants us to do, so that we will be less effective for the message of Christ. How do you share Jesus and His grace with someone when you can't receive it for yourself? You cannot lead where you will not go.

Let me encourage you today to receive the grace that is so freely offered to you through our Savior, Jesus Christ. He longs to give it to you and you need it – so what are you waiting for? Go get it and be free!

Lord,
Thank You for Your forgiveness and grace! I receive it!
Amen!

Freedom From Opinion

You were running a good race. Who cut in on you to keep you from obeying the truth? That kind of persuasion does not come from the one who calls you. Galatians 5:7-8

"Lynn, why do you care so much about what that person thinks? You belong to the Lord and you are His child! You don't answer to anyone else but Him! Let them be judgmental if they want to. You keep on doing what the Lord has called you to do!" These were wise words, from a wise woman. (Imagine them being said in a beautiful English accent. I love to hear my friend speak!)

Someone had recently been rather critical and judgmental towards me, and it didn't hurt me as much as it made me angry. I felt misunderstood and that they were being very harsh and legalistic. Why was I so concerned with what they thought?

The enemy is subtle. When we are trying to obey the Lord and serve Him, the enemy knows that he usually can't distract us with the obvious. He typically distracts us with the subtle power of persuasion.

In this particular verse, Paul asks the Galatians, "Who cut in on you to keep you from obeying the truth?" The Galatians were arguing over legalistic issues. They had taken their focus off of the grace offered to them through the cross, and had placed it on works. They were leading new Christians astray with their legalism.

Have you ever been under the influence of a "rule follower?" If you didn't do everything just right in their eyes, were you're made to feel as though you were less than? If I worry about pleasing others and trying to do everything just "right," then I have missed the boat! Rule followers can get really hung up on the little things, and forget the most important – grace. We are called to try and live a life that pleases God, not man.

Who are the voices of influence that you listen to? Are they speaking God's truth to you, or distracting you from it? In the words of Paul, "That kind of persuasion does not come from the One who calls you!" Enough said!

Lord,
Please help me to listen to Your voice above all other voices. Free me from being too concerned about trying to please others and help me to do what pleases You. Thank You for the free gift of Your Grace!
Amen.

A New Creation

Therefore, if anyone is in Christ, the new creation has come: The old has gone, the new is here! 2 Corinthians 5:17

This is a season of new beginnings for our family. On Saturday, we went to our new home to see the painter's finished product. I couldn't believe the transformation! All the colors on the walls had been dark and depressing to me. A lot of trim work was done in black and it felt heavy. The new colors were light and bright and the trim was a crisp white. Everything looked fresh and clean and it looked like a different place.

It dawned on me that this is a lot like our transformation through Christ. Before we accepted Him as Savior, our lives were dark and heavy with the weight of sin, but as a new creation in Christ our lives are transformed into something beautiful, clean and spotless.

So here is my question: Why do we sometimes live like we are not a new creation? Do you find yourself burdened with the weight of a current sin struggle or by the shame of former sin? Have we truly left our old nature behind us and taken on the new life in Christ? Are we serious about our faith or just playing church?

Maybe it's time to let go of the things that weigh us down. (See Hebrews 12) Once we have accepted Christ, there is no need to hang on to our past life – not the guilt, not the habits. Much like my new home, maybe the walls of our lives need to be repainted. Let's trade the dark heaviness of sin and shame for a new clean life of freedom in Christ Jesus.

Lord,
Thank You that You make all things new! Thank You for the freedom from sin and shame through Your Son, Jesus Christ!
Amen!

Depression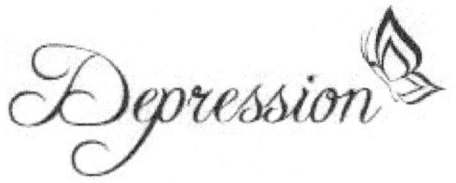

Come to the Healer.

Laughter Hides the Pain

Laughter can conceal a heavy heart, but when the laughter ends, the grief remains. Proverbs 14:13

Not many people know this fact, but I have known suicidal depression intimately. When I was almost 16, I attempted to take my life with an overdose of pills. Exactly 16 years later, when I was almost 32, I was again plagued with the constant consuming thoughts of suicide and had to be hospitalized for eight days.

The reason that many people did not know I was struggling with depression is because I put on a happy face for everyone. I covered my pain with smiles and laughter. I was embarrassed to admit my struggle, and I thought people would think I was weak. I covered it to the best of my ability, but as this Scripture says, at the end of the day, the pain was still there.

Are you hiding a pain because you are worried about what others will think? Friend, let me assure you, you are not alone. The worst thing you can do is keep your pain to yourself and allow the enemy to make you feel ashamed and hopeless.

Let me encourage you to cry out to God for help, and reach out to a trusted friend, medical professional, pastor or counselor to get the help you need. You are precious! You are fearfully and wonderfully made! The Lord Jesus died for you! He created you! He sings and dances over you! He has a plan for your life! In His Presence, you can find strength to press on if you will wholly surrender your hurt and pain to Him! Take it from someone who knows!

Lord,
For any who struggle with depression, I pray You touch them, give them strength and help them realize they are not alone. Thank You that You are our Creator, Savior and Sustainer!
Amen.

 Love
as We Have Been Loved

Love one another,
for love comes from God

We are not Orphans

No, I will not abandon you as orphans—I will come to you. John 14:18

Orphan in Greek is translated "fatherless." Other translations say "comfortless."

We live in a time when living in a fatherless home is quite the norm. If a child actually lives in a home with both of the biological parents still together, it is quite unusual and that child is considered "lucky" by their peers. Raising a granddaughter brings this issue all too close to home for Mark and me.

I just heard a presentation explaining the different programs the Florida Baptist Children's Home has put in place to try and minister to the growing needs of orphaned children in our state. It is heartbreaking to think of all the children that are homeless, abandoned and abused. This epidemic calls for our action as Christians!

As a ministry to women, we see how childhood trauma leads to spiritual bondage as adults. There are many women who have been wounded as children by the very people they should have been able to trust and depend on.

In this passage, Jesus is telling his followers that he will not abandon them as orphans. He will not leave them fatherless or comfortless. Maybe you have (or someone you know has) come from a background of deep pain due to childhood trauma. Maybe, like Mark and me, you have been called to minister to a child in need. The most important thing that must be communicated to those precious children is that

Jesus loves them and He has not, nor will He ever, abandon them! He is the father to the fatherless.

Let me encourage you to support local agencies that minister to the needs of displaced children. If you can volunteer your time, money or talents to better the life of a child, you have done a great thing for the Kingdom of God. Pray and act as the Lord leads you and may He be glorified as lives are changed.

Lord,
Thank You that you never abandon us! Please help us as believers open our eyes to the needs of those around us that have been abandoned or feel alone. Heal us from our broken places so we may be used by You to reach others for You.
Amen.

Love One Another

Dear friends, let us love one another, for love comes from God. Everyone who loves has been born of God and knows God. 1 John 4:7

Sometimes there are people in our lives that are hard to love. Their actions or words make it difficult to even like them and enjoy spending time with them.

Whatever the circumstance we face with family members, friends, co-workers, bosses, neighbors, etc., we are instructed in God's Word to love them with the love that only comes from God. In our natural human efforts we cannot love others the way we should. Our emotions get in the way. God calls us be His conduit of love to others. If we could see ourselves as the vessel by which God wants to reveal Himself to others around us, it might be a little easier to love them.

You may be dealing with people who are difficult to love. If so, remember three things: 1. God loves us unconditionally even when we are unlovely; 2. God instructs us to love others as He has loved us; 3. God is the source of love and only He can give us the ability to love others. It is simply our responsibility to ask for it.

Lord
Please help me to love others as You have loved me.
Amen.

Control
Issues

I am a control freak!

Control Freak!

Listen and give heed, do not be haughty, For the Lord has spoken.
Jeremiah 13:15

Haughty – having a feeling of superiority that shows itself in an overbearing attitude.

I feel as though I should stand up in front of a room full of my friends and family and say, "I am sorry for being such a control freak!"

It is one thing to be organized and somewhat structured in order to avoid chaos or irresponsibility, but it is another to find yourself controlling every little detail of your and your family's life.

I tend to think I am helping. If I don't do it, or take care of it, or remind them to do it, then nothing will ever get done and there will be complete chaos in the land! The plates that are spinning in the air will all come crashing down! (Is anyone with me here, or am I on this island all by myself?)

A wise person once told me to stop over-functioning for everyone – to stop thinking I have to do it all. I was recently talking about this with one of my sisters and she said I needed to learn how to just let some things go. What real difference is it going to make if something doesn't get done exactly how or when I think it ought to? The earth will not stop rotating on its axis and come to an end.

My ministry team remind me often that I need to let them do their jobs instead of trying to take everything on myself. When I try to do it all, I am taking away their opportunity to use their gifts, not using my gifts properly, and making them feel like they are not needed.

When I over-function for my family, I am communicating to my husband that I can't trust him to do anything right, and I am enabling my granddaughter to always depend on me and never feel confident to be independent. None of this is what I desire to make them feel!

I talked this issue over with my husband and told him that I really want to break this bad habit. I asked him to keep me accountable, and he was sweet to offer to take some things off my plate to help out.

I told my ministry team to remind me to back off when they see me taking on more than I should and/or trying to control things.

By nature, I am bent to be organized, neat, tidy and responsible. In business these qualities have certainly helped me. However, my father's wise words still ring in my head – our weaknesses are usually our strengths taken to an extreme. So true! These good qualities can lead to serious control issues and damage the very relationships I hold dear.

Whether we mean to or not, if we have a tendency to control or micro-manage we are guilty of having a haughty spirit. This is the sin of pride. Look at the definition above. Having a feeling of superiority – our way is the best way. Having an overbearing attitude – everyone should do it our way and if they don't they will hear about it.

Have you ever caught yourself talking down to or over someone in order to get your point across? Do you have a tendency to think your way is the best and/or the only way things should be done? Do you get angry when things don't get done your way? You may think you're helping, but you may really be hurting the very people and relationships you care about.

Allow the Lord to speak to your heart and show you the areas of your life where you need to let go of control. Humility is the opposite of haughty. You may need to apologize to friends or family for having had a haughty attitude. It may be challenging, but with the Lord's help you can do it. Take it from someone who knows – I am on the journey too!

Lord,
Please forgive me for the times I have had a haughty spirit. Please help me see when I am trying to control others and circumstances. Please help me to discern the difference between being responsible and being controlling. Thank You for Your forgiveness and restoration.
Amen.

But I Prayed About It!

Be anxious for nothing, but in everything by prayer and supplication with thanksgiving let your requests be made known to God. And the peace of God, which surpasses all comprehension, will guard your hearts and your minds in Christ Jesus. Finally, brethren, whatever is true, whatever is honorable, whatever is right, whatever is pure, whatever is lovely, whatever is of good repute, if there is any excellence and if anything worthy of praise, dwell on these things. The things you have learned and received and heard and seen in me, practice these things, and the God of peace will be with you. Philippians 4:6-9

As I listened to a friend tell me about a difficult situation she was going through, I could see that she wanted so badly to be delivered from her hurt feelings. She kept saying, "I've prayed and asked God to help me do and say the right things and move past this, but I just can't seem to do it." It dawned on me that my friend seemed to be praying and then trying to answer the prayer too. She would pray and then try to act in a way she thought she ought to. My sister once gave my daughter some great advice about praying about her circumstances, and it hit me that the same advice applied here.

My sister said, "You are praying about the situation, but you have your fingers in your ears while you're doing it. You are afraid to listen to what God is saying because it might not be what you want to hear." Powerful and very accurate advice!

We take many things to the Lord in prayer, all the while we have our ears plugged up. We stop with the petition and don't wait for the answer. If the situation doesn't change or our feelings don't change, we think God just isn't answering our prayer. We think He has a hearing problem, when actually we have the listening problem. We are spiritually hearing impaired!

Like my friend, we pray and then run off to try and fix the situation in our own power. We have ideas about how we should react, or what we should say. We analyze it to death and then run it by our closest girlfriends or family members to see what they think. We listen to so many voices rather than to the One Voice that truly matters.

Have you been praying about something and you haven't felt like you have received an answer? Are you full of anxiety, worry, fear, anger, bitterness, jealousy, etc.? Could it possibly be because your fingers are in your ears when you pray?

In Philippians 4:6-9, Paul instructs believers to not worry about anything, but to pray about everything. He goes on to say that this is the way to experience peace. When the troubles around us begin to make us anxious or cause us to worry, we should stop that pattern of thinking in its tracks and start praying.

You see, God's peace is not found in positive, self-help thinking. It is found in the knowledge that God is in control. He knows what we need and He will provide it, in His time, and in His way. We should let that knowledge and assurance wash over us. May it guard our hearts and minds against anything that threatens to steal God's peace from us.

Lord,

Please help me to listen when I pray. Help me to keep my ears unplugged and to accept whatever answer You give. Stop me in my tracks if I start trying to handle the situation myself. Thank You that You are in control and I don't have to be. Amen.

Weary

He gives strength
to the weary.

Exhausted

I am exhausted from crying for help; my throat is parched. My eyes are swollen with weeping, waiting for my God to help me. Psalm 69:3

Have you ever cried until you were literally exhausted? There are many different reasons why this can happen. Sometimes it is due to the loss of a loved one, a betrayal by someone you trusted, or challenging circumstances that seem impossible to bear.

There have been many mornings when I have had to put cold compresses on my eyes and slather on a pound of eye cream to battle the swelling. Has there ever been a time when you were heartbroken over the stronghold of sin in your life? While recognizing and repenting of our sin is a necessary and very cathartic process, be careful to not let it lead to guilt and shame. The enemy would love nothing more than to paralyze you in moving forward in your walk and work with the Lord by using shame and guilt.

The weight of the burdens of this life can easily make us weary. It is at those times that we must pursue the Father with intentional purpose. Get on your face and cry out to Him, pouring out your heart until it is empty and wait on Him to answer. He will provide – He will help.

Lord,
Thank You for Your comfort in my times of distress. Thank You for Your forgiveness and direction in my life, no matter the circumstances around me.
Amen

Spiritual Exercise

Consider it pure joy, my brothers and sisters, whenever you face trials of many kinds, because you know that the testing of your faith produces perseverance. Let perseverance finish its work so that you may be mature and complete, not lacking anything. James 1:2-4

I don't know about you, but I really don't like trials. Actually, I despise them. Yet, this Scripture tells me to consider them pure joy. What?! Pure joy…are you kidding me?!

The trials mentioned here are not trials brought on by temptations or sin; these are trials that test our faith. These are the trials that stretch us, mold us and shape us into who God has called us to be in order to fulfill what He has called us to do. They are like spiritual exercise.

Have you ever started working out and your muscles ached the next day so badly it hurt to move? Your muscles are being stretched and developed. The pain is part of the process of reaching the physical goal of fitness. Just like trials, I hate the pain of exercise. Unfortunately, in both cases the pain is part of the growth and development. Have you ever noticed that the times we grow the most in our spiritual walk is when we are going through a trial?

James is encouraging us to persevere in our trials, so that we may finish the work God has for us to do here on earth. He goes on to explain that this maturing of our faith helps us to become complete and lacking nothing. This means that we will have everything we need to be an effective witness for Christ and able to withstand the temptations of the evil one.

Mark and I have been going through a personal trial in our family lately. We are most certainly being tested. Joy is not the first word that comes to my mind when we think about this trial. However, we have realized that we don't believe we are to be joyful about the trial itself, but rather the spiritual fruit it will produce in us as we go through it.

If you are facing a particularly challenging trial, I pray you will find some comfort and peace in this verse in James. The old saying, "No pain, no gain" is quite appropriate. We must realize that we are being refined in order to complete the work God has for us. May we not grow weary in our perseverance!

Lord,
Please give me the strength to persevere, so that I may be made complete.
Amen.

We are Weak, but He is Strong

He gives strength to the weary and increases the power of the weak.
Isaiah 40:29

"I am so tired!" These were my words to my husband as I dropped into the bed. It had been a tough day! Early morning phone calls regarding important business matters – very busy day at work – home at 6:00 and immediately start dinner – listen and comfort our teenager over hurt feelings by a friend – check email – check my "to do" list – wash my face – fall into bed exhausted. The next day appeared to be just as busy. I thought, Lord, how do I keep going?! I am so tired!

As I read this verse, I realized that the Lord will supply His power according to my need, and He will give me the strength to do what I must do each and every day.

Sometimes, I don't feel like talking to anyone on the phone, answering email, cooking dinner or listening to teenage drama. I grow weary! It is at those times that I must ask God for strength. There are times we can – and need – to take a time-out! We can screen calls, check email later, order a pizza and let our husband deal with the children's needs. However, there are times when we can't.

We're needed by a friend who is going through a difficulty. Time sensitive business emails must be tended to. Your family needs a good home cooked meal, and your children need some quality time with you. This is when the Lord does some of His most amazing work. Somehow, He gives us the strength to get it all done.

Are you tired? Are you feeling weary? Claim this verse and ask the Lord to give you all that you need to fulfill all that He has called you to do today. When you wake the next day – ask again. This is a moment by moment need. We are weak, but He is strong!

Lord,
Thank You for giving me the strength I need to do all that You have called me to do today. May I not try to do it in my own power or take on more than what You have asked me to do. Anoint me with Your power and turn my weakness into a testimony of Your provision.
Amen.

Sorrow

My help comes from
the Lord!

Technical Difficulties!

For I reckon that the sufferings of this present time are not worthy to be compared with the glory which shall be revealed to us-ward. Romans 8:18

The term "technical difficulties" seems very appropriate for life right now. We have personally had several technical issues since we moved. However, there have been other issues of life that have caused a little aggravation lately – or as my granddaughter used to say, "aggrabate'in."

Life is full of aggravations and challenges. The question is: Will we let those overshadow the joy of knowing Christ and looking forward to what is coming? Have we forgotten that this life is very temporary?

I love this verse and it came to me while I was blow-drying my hair this morning. I was a little aggravated – ok, a lot aggravated – about several little things. I know the Lord sent this verse to my mind in order to help me turn my focus back where it needed to be.

The phrase "to us-ward" actually means Christ's Glory revealed in Heaven to us, on us and in us. Therefore, our minds should be primarily focused on the Glory of Christ being revealed in Heaven when we see Him face to face. The very thought of that should make everything in this life quickly fade. This verse tells us that the struggles or sufferings of this life are not even worthy of being compared to Christ's Glory.

One of the many things I love about this verse is that it uses a familiar southern expression – "reckon." My family (and most certainly my husband's family) has used that word for as long as I can remember. It actually means: **to consider, to think or suppose. (Webster's Dictionary)**

So, if life is throwing you some technical difficulties that are "aggrabate'in" you, I reckon you should turn your focus to the Glory of Christ revealed to us, on us and in us in Heaven. Amen?

Lord,
Thank You for helping me focus on what matters. The day I see You face to face in all Your Glory is my deepest desire! Please help me to remember that and let the issues of this life fade away.
Amen.

Strength for Our Sorrows

My soul melts away for sorrow; strengthen me according to your word!
Psalm 119:28

In one day, I had a client whose husband suddenly died, another struggling as a caregiver, and a teen who feels abandoned by her father because she hasn't heard from him in almost two months. These are just a few of the stories of pain and sorrow I often encounter in a day. You can probably think of many more in your circle of family, friends and co-workers. Maybe you are one of these stories – someone who is carrying a heavy load.

It is my deepest desire to do something to ease the pain I see in each face. Scripture reminds us that this is not our home – Praise God! These sufferings are only for a while, but sometimes the grief and sorrow can grip our hearts and minds to the point we physically ache.

I believe the Psalmist expresses it well. He feels as if his very soul is wasting away from sorrow. His only hope is to find strength in God's Word.

If we are not currently going through a struggle, then we may not feel the sense of urgency to read God's Word. However, God's Word also prepares us for encounters we will have with people who need an encouraging, timely and discerning word. If we have been with the Lord in fellowship through His Word and prayer, we are being prepared for what and who we will face that day. Being in God's Word isn't always about what we get out of it for ourselves, but also what we can share with others.

If you are struggling with a particular pain or sorrow, let me encourage you to spend time talking to the Lord and telling Him how you feel. Read His Word for the purpose of finding strength to carry on and knowing that this world (and all its sorrows) is not our home.

Lord,
Thank You for Your strength You give in our times of need. Please comfort us and give us peace. Heal our broken hearts as only You can. Amen.

My Help Comes From the Lord!

I lift up my eyes to the hills. From where does my help come? My help comes from the Lord, who made heaven and earth. He will not let your foot be moved; he who keeps you will not slumber. Behold, he who keeps Israel will neither slumber nor sleep. The Lord is your keeper; the Lord is your shade on your right hand. The sun shall not strike you by day, nor the moon by night. The Lord will keep you from all evil; he will keep your life. The Lord will keep your going out and your coming in from this time forth and forevermore. Psalm 121:1-8

This passage is one of my favorites. There are several promises in this Psalm.

1. When I am in need, my Lord (The Creator of heaven and earth – my Savior) is my help. You can't get better or greater help than that!

2. He keeps my steps secure. He won't let me fall.

3. He does not sleep. He isn't going to get caught "sleeping on the job." He is always aware and watching over me. Nothing catches Him by surprise.

4. He is my Keeper – my Comforter – my Protector.

5. He is always with me as I come and go about my day. He is with me forever.

I take great comfort in these promises. I pray today that you read this Psalm and as you meditate on it, let the Lord speak to your heart. Rest in the knowledge that your help comes from the Lord.

Lord,
Thank You for being with me every moment in every situation. Thank You for Your help that is all sufficient for my every need.
Amen.

Feeling Overwhelmed?

From the end of the earth, I will call to you, when my heart is overwhelmed. Lead me to the rock that is higher than I. Psalm 61:2

Do you ever wake up feeling overwhelmed? Maybe you feel overwhelmed by all that you know is facing you today. There are times that the daily chores and errands can seem like a never ending task.

There is an endless list of burdens that can also leave us feeling overwhelmed. (i.e., illness, caregiving, grief, marital stress, divorce, desire to be married, infertility, the challenges of raising children, financial difficulties, career/job stress, an area of sin or shame, etc.)

Recently, I was praying about several issues I have been facing. I told the Lord that I was overwhelmed. As I continued to pray, I felt the Lord speak to my mind and ask me, "Lynn, why are you overwhelmed with the circumstances you are facing, when you should be overwhelmed by My presence in your life and My power to handle anything you face?" That was a humbling moment!

I realized that my focus had been on the problems and not the Problem Solver! I asked the Lord to help me rest in the knowledge that He was in control and that He would provide. I asked Him to give me His peace.

This does not mean that I don' t feel all of the normal human emotions that come with the challenges of this life. The difference is, I don't have to live consumed by them. My emotions don't have to be in control of me, but rather through God's power, I am in control of them.

In the International Standard Version of Psalm 61:2 it says, "Lead me to the rock that is too high for me." In essence, lead me to a place I cannot reach without you.

This makes me think of the old saying, "Under the circumstances…" God calls us to live above the circumstances. He calls us to the high places where only He can take us. This is where we can begin to see things from a heavenly perspective rather than an earthly one.

Lord,
I pray today that no matter what we face, You will take us to the rock that is higher than we could ever reach, and that You will set our feet upon it and give us peace. May we no longer be overwhelmed by the burdens of this life, but rather overwhelmed by Your presence and provision.
Amen.

It's Gonna' Get Better

He will wipe every tear from their eyes. There will be no more death or mourning or crying or pain, for the old order of things has passed away.
Revelation 21:4

In this passage, we are given a description of what it will be like when Christ returns and there is a new Heaven and a new Earth. I don't know about you, but I am looking forward to what this verse describes! No more pain, sorrow, mourning or death! I cannot wait!

Every time you turn on the news, there is calamity everywhere. It seems as though I hear about pain and suffering from friends almost daily. Recently, someone dear to me was diagnosed with breast cancer and today, another person I once was rather close to suddenly died.

As Christians, how do we maintain a level of joy when we see and experience so much tragedy? The answer – because of the hope that is within us through Christ Jesus, our Lord! (See Romans)

This is our temporary home. Our eternal home is in Heaven with Christ. The whole earth groans for (longs for) Christ's return. Until that day comes, we must hold on to The Hope that is within us and persevere. We must share the message of Christ with everyone we possibly can. Time is drawing nigh.

If you are in a season of suffering – hang in there – The Lord is coming – all things will be made new and there will be no more pain. Cry out to the Lord and ask for His strength to get you through. Ask Him to give you His joy and peace.

Sometimes there are great lessons learned in the midst of sorrow.

When I was a child, I fell down and scraped my knee pretty badly. I still remember it and I have a small scar on my right knee to this day. My father was the best at doctoring my scrapes and cuts. On this particular occasion, my dad rinsed it and dabbed it – while I cried with vigor. Dad put Mercurochrome on it (which was considered the magic medicine) and a nice big band-aide. He gave me a Kleenex and got me calmed down a bit and then he said, "You know what?" I said, "What?" He replied, with his smirky smile, "It's gonna' feel better when it quits hurting." It took me a minute, but then I started laughing at his cute attempt at humor.

To this day, I think about that when I am going through something painful. In the middle of my cry-fest I suddenly realize that this is only a season, and with God's help I am going to get through it. My mother often says, "Lynn, this too shall pass."

We will go through adversity, but we need to take heart and realize that one day all of the pain of this world will be over. It will feel better and it won't hurt anymore.

Lord,
Thank You for Your strength to get through each day. Thank You that You have given us a future and a hope. May we shine the light of Christ to those around us so that they will be drawn to You. We look forward to the day when we will be with You in Heaven and there will be no more pain and suffering. Until that day comes, Lord comfort us, strengthen us, heal us, protect us and guide us.
Amen.

Patience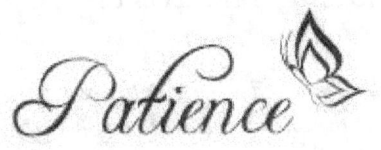

The Lord is coming!

Be Patient, The Lord is Coming!

Be patient, then, brothers and sisters, until the Lord's coming. See how the farmer waits for the land to yield its valuable crop, patiently waiting for the autumn and spring rains. You too, be patient and stand firm, because the Lord's coming is near. James 5:7-8

Do you sometimes feel your patience is being tested? After having a long conversation with a friend I hadn't talked to in a while, I was amazed at how much adversity she and her husband were enduring. She said their faith was strong, but their patience was being tested. That made complete sense to me.

Have you ever told your children or grandchildren to be patient. They are typically in a hurry for everything to happen right now! Instant gratification is the message of this world and they have heard it well. We are not much different as believers. When God asks for us to wait patiently we get frustrated. It is hard for us to stand firm and remember the Lord is in control – He is near – He is coming – and He will act in His timing.

If something isn't happening fast enough to suit us, we grow weary and frustrated. We think God isn't listening or He doesn't care. Nothing could be further from the truth! He has a purpose in the timing.

This passage reminds us that Christ is coming back one day and all of the trials of this world will be over. We must stand firm in our faith and wait patiently for Him.

Like my friend, you may be in a season where your patience is being tested. Do not fret. The Lord's coming is near - and He is always on time!

Lord,
Thank You that You are always near and that Your timing is perfect.
Please help me stand firm and be patient in the waiting.
Amen.

RESOURCES

The Bible versions used in this devotional book:

New International Version
New Living Translation
English Standard Version
New American Standard
King James
Matthew Henry's Concise Commentary
Strong's Exhaustive Concordance
Tyndale Life Application Study Bible NLT Commentary Webster's
Online Dictionary

www.ingramcontent.com/pod-product-compliance

Lightning Source LLC
Chambersburg PA
CBHW052048070526

44584CB00017B/2104